INNOVATION WARS

INNOVATION WARS

*Driving Successful
Corporate Innovation
Programs*

SCOTT BALES

NEW YORK

LONDON • NASHVILLE • MELBOURNE • VANCOUVER

INNOVATION WARS
Driving Successful Corporate Innovation Programs

© 2019 **SCOTT BALES**

Published in New York, New York, by Morgan James Publishing. Morgan James is a trademark of Morgan James, LLC. www.MorganJamesPublishing.com

ISBN 978-1-64279-240-9 paperback
ISBN 978-1-64279-241-6 eBook
ISBN 978-1-64279-242-3 hardcover
Library of Congress Control Number: 2018910416

Cover Design by:
Rachel Lopez
www.r2cdesign.com

Interior Design by:
Bonnie Bushman
The Whole Caboodle Graphic Design

In an effort to support local communities, raise awareness and funds, Morgan James Publishing donates a percentage of all book sales for the life of each book to Habitat for Humanity Peninsula and Greater Williamsburg.

Get involved today! Visit
www.MorganJamesBuilds.com

DEDICATION

To Jenson, Luca and Kai,
my greatest teachers in life.

TABLE OF CONTENTS

FOREWORD

In business, there is a word that nobody speaks about—a four-letter word.

When I was young, I felt that I was the only person who struggled with this. As I lay awake at night or walked out of difficult meetings, after we lost an important contract or a critical debtor just did not pay on time—in instances where a key employee resigned or important projects ran late and did not deliver on time. I thought I was unique and that others just knew how to manage in these difficult situations and I could not. I was often confronted by this word:

FEAR

Fear is debilitating—it stifles performance and innovation. It stops us from taking the next step or break out of our constrained thinking. It makes us feel tired and as if we are lost. Yet, there is nothing that was ever created without someone confronting his or her own fear. It is scary to break with tradition or to wander off the well-known trail. The only way to do this in a radical way is to recognize our fear and deal with it.

We do not speak enough about fear.

This is why this book is so important. There are many books that explain the process of finding inspiration and getting fresh ideas, but Scott confronts the emotion of innovation in this book. He thinks about, and explains, the importance of a personal journey—why innovation wars are not really about new ideas, but about people who have to execute on them.

He must be complimented that he broke the mold of traditional books, guiding each of us to confront our own fear, to harness it so that we can win in the new innovation wars.

—**Hannes van Rensburg**, CEO & Founder, Fundamo
Fundamo provides mobile financial solutions for banks,
financial organizations and mobile network operators.
It was acquired by VISA for $110 million.

Introduction
TWO SIDES OF THE COIN

"Innovation distinguishes between a leader and a follower."
—Steve Jobs

In 2008, my life changed forever. I was thrown into the deep end of entrepreneurial life in a small Southeast Asian country of Cambodia. I'd worked for some years for the Australian and New Zealand Banking Group (ANZ Bank), a large Australia-based multinational company that operates in more than 34 markets. What seemed at first to be a routine corporate initiative quickly become my most exciting and career changing experience, as I became involved in a venture with the mandate to launch an entirely new subsidiary brand and to pursue an entirely new customer set.

I remember getting off the plane, feeling excited at the challenge a role in a new country offered, little realizing it would completely change my professional life. Taking up a new challenge like this was a bit like going into battle. It's a metaphor that's stayed with me. And like all Samurai warriors, I have my Samurai code.

I'm going to delve into my time in Cambodia (and other places) throughout this book, and tell a little of my own innovation journey along the way, but suffice to say since that transformative time in my life I've become deeply embedded in the world of startups and tech. You could say innovation is in my blood. Since then, I've used all that I've learned and applied various experimental methods to create businesses from the ground up. Simply put, I have had the unique and personally gratifying experience to see innovation from both the corporate and startup worlds.

The experiences I went through gave me a gift: to see how both of these ecospheres move, create, and build products and enterprises—and I have discovered one hugely important insight: the two can actually learn from each other.

Traditional companies, for example, tend to be stuck in their ways, and could acquire a great deal from understanding how innovative and lean startup-oriented businesses rapidly ideate and validate ideas. Most of all, larger businesses can discover how these concepts can make them more competitive in an age increasingly defined and driven by technology, from social media to app development and mobility.

On the flip side of the coin, entrepreneurs and startups have the opportunity to delve deeper into the universe of traditional companies and find out how they are able to maintain stability and success after so many years of operation. It is time to let our startups become more scalable, sustainable, and global in every aspect, whether in the areas of marketing, branding, administration or finance. Some things don't need to be reinvented.

I am not trying to say that both of these groups have to cross over, but that each can be a great teacher to the other, so all participants can be competitive, ready to tackle the challenges of the future and create vibrant, sustainable offerings to markets and consumers around the world.

We live in an interesting time, for sure. No company's safe, no matter its size. While seemingly invincible corporations have fallen to the armies of much smaller companies, the list of small companies defeated (or swallowed up) by larger corporates is much longer still.

Going back to my metaphor, and the theme of this book: Why "war"? Is this the right analogy to describe what's happening in the realm of innovation?

I believe that it is, and it's a war that needs to be fought on multiple fronts. There is the front of the known enemy—the direct competitor. There is also the front of the unknown competitor—the unforeseen or as yet unemerged startup with a bold new idea. And there is the internal front, the battle against a company culture and structure that is resistant to change. In this multi-pronged environment, incumbent companies need to start getting serious about their strategy for fighting this innovation war if they intend to survive.

"We know that the nation that goes all-in on innovation today will own the global economy tomorrow. This is an edge America cannot surrender." So said President Obama in his 2014 State of the Union Address: It was almost fighting talk, from a President who had done his best to remove America from conflict. It emphasizes the importance of innovation to business and to the global economy. You cannot come second in the innovation space. History is littered with losers, and also-ran inventions (HD-DVD vs BluRay?) Success brings great financial success, and most of the time there can be only one winner. There's just one Uber (that anyone uses).

What to do? Again, here the war analogy is an apt one. To win, a company must have the right innovation soldiers filling its ranks. These soldiers in turn must be trained correctly and have the right skills. They must be supplied with the right equipment. The right tools to do their job. You need the right allies in the fight. Most of all you need to make sure they're in the right environment, on the right battlefield. It would have been no good if the Duke of Wellington's army had made for the Battle of Waterloo but ended up in Antwerp instead.

Defeat looms large on the corporate battleground. "Innovate or die" is the constant battle cry. Big companies that fail to innovate certainly risk extinction. That's the stark truth in the era of digital disruption. They can't remain neutral. Sit and do nothing is no longer an option. Commodore Computers, Woolworths, Kodak, Borders, and Pan Am all tried business-as-usual—and failed.

So what to do? How exactly does a company become more innovative? "Innovation" has itself become a bit of a buzzword that managers and CEOs bandy around without grasping what it means, with even less clue about how to actually implement a successful innovation program. Do you just need to engage with consumers more? Do you just need some funky furniture and a room to "brainstorm" in?

I wrote this book with a couple of goals in mind, firstly to create a collaborative dialogue for both legacy and startup businesses to embrace the idea of consumer empowerment; something is changing the very nature of business. In the end, businesses continue—and may cease—to exist purely on their ability to connect with the demands of the market. It is time for all, especially for legacy companies, to harness technologies and models that allow them to build better relationships among customers across demographics and product categories. The future of organizations lies in their ability to create collaborative learning from each other for the good of consumers whose needs are ever changing but continuously have to be addressed.

The word "startup" has rocketed into mainstream by becoming a buzzword synonymous with high tech, rapid innovation, and disruptive businesses. Right across the globe there is a strong desire for people to build their own empire, creating platforms or technologies that alter the course of industries, or make the world a better place. Competitions, challenges and hackathons such as Startup Weekend have carved strong reputations as the launching pad for the next Steve Jobs or Mark Zuckerberg.

All this excitement, passion and hype runs in the face of the staggering odds against the chance of success. In parallel, these innovative methods, frameworks and toolsets are quickly finding their way inside large organizations. A perfect example is the evolution of the "lean startup" model over the past five years. What started as a methodology for increasing efficiency and productivity while reducing costs and time has become the new approach to corporate innovation. The lean methods are powerful, by focusing on building and marketing only products the market is willing to buy, thus avoiding the embarrassing losses of investment in products nobody wants. Traditional companies to date have not typically adopted the ideas of disruptive innovation and lean startups, preferring to follow the same traditions, cultures, and methodologies that have been passed on from one management team to another. But an air of change is wafting its way into the corporate world, as more and more startup ideas are being trialed.

Secondly, I want to give you, the reader, business owners and managers, or perhaps startup entrepreneurs, some insights from my own innovation experience, and provide a framework of concepts, a battle plan, if you like that will help you along the path to implementing innovation within your own organization. Over the past few years the demand for my expertise in Lean has shifted. Well not really shifted, it's more like the corporate world has woken up. These days I spend large amounts of time helping heads of innovation build new capabilities, frameworks, and to experiment with ideas that don't quite fit their traditional initiatives processes. It's become the new battlefront, as large organizations arm themselves with tools, skills, and approaches normally left to the world of startups.

What to Expect From This Book

This book is meant as a guidebook to innovation for any business leader who's struggling to establish a culture of innovation within their organization. This struggle is especially acute at many medium and large companies, where entrenched corporate culture, habits, and processes make it difficult to "stir the pot" and drive true disruption.

This book will first situate the reader by discussing the roots of innovation back to the start of the Industrial Era. We'll then look at examples of companies that have stood out in the modern era and the present day for their ability to innovate at scale—large corporations like Google and Apple that manage to behave in many ways like a startup—as well as previously world-beating companies whose past success has hindered them from seeing the dangers and opportunities that come with rapid change. We'll also explore how the democratization of several key technologies, and even of education itself, is changing the playing field of innovation, as well as how the growing cadre of digital natives are serving as the armies in numerous companies' battle to innovate in the 21st century.

The core value of this book, however, lies in Parts 3 and 4, where I provide an in-depth overview of my own recipe for success in winning an innovation war. It's a recipe cultivated over a decade of helping companies drive innovation in the financial services sector and many other industries. Through this experience, I've identified four key elements that every aspiring, innovative company needs to possess, as well as four traits that every individual who seeks to become more innovative needs to develop. This framework, termed the 4Cs and the 4Ps, provides a holistic blueprint for innovation, as it takes into account the requirements at both the company and individual level for an organization to triumph in their innovation war.

My aim with this book is to give you a powerful starting point for winning your innovation war—the background, the tools, and the frameworks to successfully facilitate innovation within your companies. I hope it provides you motivation and direction for the battles ahead.

PART 1

LOOKING BACK:
THE HISTORY OF INNOVATION

Chapter 1

INNOVATION, FROM ROOTS TO SHOOTS

I t's often said that "history repeats itself." However, the truth may be closer to the idea that "history rhymes."

We must learn from the past to understand how to navigate the future. We cannot look to the past to understand exactly *what* will happen in the future because the future is almost guaranteed to unfold in ways we cannot predict, to produce technologies, ideas, and business models we can't currently conceive. But we can use it to understand *how* the future *might* unfold—to see the shape and pattern of inevitable change. And we can also use it to to help us navigate and yes, *innovate* toward that future.

By understanding the constant nature of change, as well as how companies have either thrived by embracing change and innovation, or stagnated when they haven't, we can get some clues about how companies in the 21st century need to think about innovation and how they can arm themselves to confront this unavoidable challenge.

I want to begin by looking back into the past, at the history of innovation, and the development of the traditional company that we know today, because the roots of corporate innovation began with the rise of the Industrial Era.

It's important to know the lessons of the past, and there have been incredible successes and vast failures, in order to learn from them.

Etymology: Invention vs. Innovation

To uncover the history of innovation, let's first take a look at the history of the word, because even in that there's evolution.

The first form of the word: "novation" began as a thirteenth century contractual term and actually meant "newness." In religious circles the word had a slight negative connotation. New ideas were not welcomed with open arms in the Puritan Era. It was practically interchangeable with "heretic"!

It wasn't until the industrial revolution that the prefix was added and "innovation" began to be associated with science and creation. It was therefore less likely to get you burned at the stake, and yet was still interchangeable with "invention." In 1912 a definition was offered by Austrian-American social scientist Joseph Schumpeter (1883–1950) that contrasted invention as being the creation of something new, while innovation was taking an invention and finding use for it inside a business model.

Schumpeter went on to disagree with the contemporary view that the economic system was an essentially passive, stationary process: "I felt very strongly that this was wrong, and that there was a source of energy within the economic system which would of itself disrupt any equilibrium that might be attained."

The "energy" he was discussing back in 1912 that disrupts the status quo, was of course innovation.

The Innovative Company in the Industrial Era

The era of the Industrial Revolution began in the 18th century. To put it simply, during the Industrial Era, everything got a lot bigger. Including businesses. The modern form of the company we recognize today *really is* less than 150 years old. You can dig deep into the history books and find other entities that *resembled* companies, and a few that might have even been termed "companies." But most pre-Industrial Era "companies" were formed by royal charter and for defined periods of time. Afterward, they would be dissolved and disappear! Part of the reason for this was these companies were often project based—they were created to undertake large, expensive infrastructure projects such as bridges or railroads, particularly in the industrial expansion of the United States.

It's probably worth noting (while we're talking history) that many writers on the subject offer a three-phase model of the history of the corporation, which goes something like this: the *Mercantilist/Smithian Era* from 1600 to 1800, the *Industrial/Schumpeterian Era* from 1800 to 2000, and finally, the era we are entering, which for want of a better name has been dubbed *the Information Era*.

The Mercantilist Era was focused on trade, and was dominated for much of this time by the Dutch East India Company. As the name of the East India Company might not suggest, the company was a *global* trading phenomenon. Some think corporations have too much political power today, but that is nothing compared to the power wielded by this beast. The Dutch East India Company had its own *army*. Its *merchant* ships had more firepower than many naval fleets. Its political and economic influence was vast. Imagine a cross between Walmart, the United States Army, and the Mafia, and you begin to get a picture of the East India Company. At its peak it was valued at roughly $7.4 trillion in today's money, making it the largest company in history.

The Dutch East India Company became that large and powerful by being innovative—by doing something no company had done before that. What it did was something familiar to us today, but at the time was unheard of: It was the first publicly traded company—the first to go public on the world's first stock exchange. This innovation allowed the company to amass enormous amounts of capital that allowed it to become the dominant force it was.

But all things change, and even the might of the Dutch East India Company finally succumbed to this process. The company lasted for 200 years, but in the end, competition, high debt, lack of capital, and the Fourth Anglo-Dutch War of 1780-1784 left the company in financial ruins. The company was nationalized in 1796, and its charter expired in 1799.

The following Industrial Era was much more focused on making products and saw the rise of the more restrained corporations that we would recognize today: focused on production, sales, marketing, and innovation, and less involved in putting hits on business opponents.

It's certainly true that the growth of the United States as a nation, mirroring the growth of the company was no accident. The development of this immense country required the construction of vast infrastructure, and the company was the perfect entity to be able to accomplish just that.

In this new environment, where physical distance became more significant given the immensity of this new nation, and as productivity levels grew, new forms of management and structure were required to drive these new business engines. Traditional hierarchies and structures were put in place to manage the accelerated production needs of the modern company.

The 1920s saw a shift in which many companies restructured from monolithic, functional organizations (sales, marketing, manufacturing, purchasing, etc.) into division-based entities (by product, territory, brand, etc.) that each had their own responsibility for profit and loss.

This model is the company we know today: an organization working within divisions to continuously improve a current business model by the incremental improvement of existing services or the introduction of new ones. It has also been a hugely successful model.

But with all the advances made since the beginning of the twentieth century, has the evolution of organizational design kept up with technological advancement, cultural, and behavioral evolution, and the rise of the informed consumer through the information age? I suggest to you that it hasn't. Continuing to improve upon existing business models will no longer be enough in coming years—with many of the great successes of the past five years demonstrating the invention of *new* business models.

In 2015, strategist Tom Goodwin astutely pointed out how these new business models represent a radical departure from previous conceptions of how companies operate, noting how:

- The largest travel company owns no real estate; Airbnb
- The largest transport company owns not a single vehicle; Uber
- The largest content company, doesn't produce a single piece of content; Facebook
- The largest retailer, holds zero inventory; Alibaba

Today, almost no industry has escaped the transformational nature of the digital shift as we enter the Information Era, resulting in some superpowers disappearing, some thriving, and others barely limping forward. That transformation hasn't stopped, and the pressures of the digital enablement of society are only getting deeper. This new world can be scary, particularly when leaders of the business world don't fully understand the possibilities, nature, and risks of the new world. It could be argued that many boardrooms are reminiscent today of Xerox circa 1979, having the future right there, in their hands, but not being able to see it. "Xerox could have owned the entire computer industry today," said Steve Jobs, commenting on the narrow vision of the then executives. "It could have been ten times its size."

In 1997, Clayton Christensen wrote *The Innovator's Dilemma*, now a cult book in the innovation community. The powerful message that Clay brought to light was that our past successes limited our future potential, and blinded us from threats we don't understand, leaving us full of excuses to justify a lack of progress. Almost every single company I meet with today is structured, positioned, and incentivized NOT to transform. Like a blind man, dependent on the support of others, a large majority of industry incumbents seek the escape of weak excuses like regulation, peer comparison, business cases, and risk avoidance, all in the hopes of distancing themselves from the fact that the world around them is changing.

How many times have you been frustrated with the technologies, process or rules of your organization? How many have had an idea on how to improve your company or industry? How far did that idea progress? My guess is not very far. Your idea faces an uphill battle through a deeply diligent process, or faces budget constraints when compared to other projects in the pipeline. Today almost every company I see has collected a pool of frustrated individuals who can see consumer technology startups doing exactly things that they know to be great opportunities, but are held back by the structure and culture of their organization.

It should be no great surprise that evolution occurs best in nature in an ideal environment. Far greater biodiversity exists in a reef system just a few kilometers away from shore in the deep ocean. Why? The reef system has been shown to require greater specialization, and over time in such places the right specialists have indeed evolved to fill the demands of the environment. Innovation, in a similar way, also requires the correct environment.

Creating a culture that suppresses new ideas in the face of uncertainty, risk, and status-quo threats is not the way forward. Our past successes hold us back from realizing the potential of future success, and this in turn opens the door, and rolls out the red carpet for disruptive innovators to wipe away market dominators or even entire industries. As was the case for Borders, Blockbuster, Kodak, Encyclopedia Britannica, and many others.

So here we are on the verge of the next era of business transformation. One that will change the rules of business forever. Change is inevitable. We just need to know where to look, and how to respond.

Chapter 2
THE ASSEMBLY LINE OF INNOVATION

W e ended the first chapter by talking about the inevitability of change. It's the organizations that accept and embrace this fact that are able to succeed in their own wars of innovation. With that in mind, let's take a look at two modern companies that have continued to succeed on the backs of such an embrace.

Ford: Back into the Black

$17 *billion* in losses. A twenty-year market share decline. A $1.90 stock price. A "cage fighting" culture. Massive layoffs. Betting the company on a $23 billion loan.

"I'm right," says incoming CEO Alan Mulally. "Ford's problems aren't as bad as Boeing's. They are much, much worse"

Mulally's in his office with Jim Morgan, a consultant who was brought in as Director of Global Body Exterior, Safety, and SBU Engineering at the Ford Motor Company in 2004. A photograph of founder Henry Ford looms high on the wall over proceedings. The company created by the entrepreneurial giant over one hundred years ago is in deep trouble. What can save it?

Morgan says one word: "Innovation."

But can a company that has been around so long still be innovative?

The Ford Motor Company certainly had its challenges in the past, even during—especially during—Henry Ford's era. Ford's first motor company failed. The company that followed didn't exactly begin with a customer-focused, innovative attitude. Ford's famous quote: "Any customer can have a car painted any color that he wants so long as it is black," was purely to avoid production bottlenecks. Black dried quicker than colors.

Innovation occurred through necessity. The company began producing just a few cars a day, but soon developed the assembly-line technique for motor vehicle production, which was initially necessary because of the increased production volume increase, but quickly became the industry norm.

Henry Ford offered profit sharing with workers when he quickly became aware of the lost profit, extra training costs, and delays associated with high staff turnover. Ford solved the turnover problem by innovating. He also doubled pay to five dollars a day and cut the nine-hour workday to eight. Everyone was happy. Staff turnover plunged, and productivity increased.

The Ford Motor Company was a corporate behemoth that continued to innovate practices through the 20th century. So what had happened by the 2000s?

Twenty years of intense competition from overseas manufacturers had left the big three of the American automotive industry in dire straits. The popularity of the SUV market kept the dogs at bay for a while, but soon the likes of Toyota began to chip away at that, too. It would take a massive bail-out to save General Motors, and Chrysler would eventually be sold to Fiat.

Ford's predicament was not as dire, but it was still significant. Although the company did not need a bailout under the TARP program, they accepted a much-needed $6 billion loan package to stay afloat. But in spite of this necessary cash infusion, Ford would have had no chance of surviving much longer without a radical shift in the way it was doing business.

Loan or no loan, for Ford it was innovate or die.

Under the guidance of Mulally and Morgan, Ford developed a strategy to ride out the turmoil and emerge stronger from it. This was achieved largely on the strength of a revitalized product line. The problems with Ford's product offerings before then were multidimensional, and the solution was incremental improvement in all areas. Ford wasn't going to go out and reinvent the wheel, but they had to make the wheel (and the entire car) better. They needed to become more cost competitive, make a leap in quality standards, and get their products to market in a much timelier manner. Everything had to be a little better than the competition so they could deliver a best-in-the-world end product.

Lean product development became the answer, and a large part of that solution was treating knowledge as capital. Harking back to founder Henry Ford's recognition of the importance of valuing people, Jim Morgan said: "It is your people that provide the skills, energy, and creativity. They are the single most important element of great product development systems. They drive the system."

Morgan led a sustained effort to reinvent automotive body and stamping development at the company. He'd published a groundbreaking research paper on the Toyota Product Development System in 1996, and this became the blueprint for his work at Ford. But his goal wasn't simply to copy Toyota's framework. "Toyota served as our inspiration, but we wanted to maintain and extend our own strengths, and we wanted to better leverage our incredibly talented people and make better use of our technology," said Morgan.

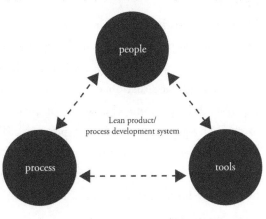

THE LEAN PRODUCT DEVELOPMENT SYSTEM AT FORD

Mutually supportive & aligned elements

Think of lean product development as a triangle with three sides: skilled people, process, and tools and technology—all working together in synergy. Morgan considered all three elements to be essential for Ford's turnaround.

Skilled People

In many traditional technology companies, managers tend to come from managerial backgrounds or lose their technical skills after they become managers. Not so anymore at Ford. Morgan recognized that when it comes to the vital people aspect of management, there was no substitute for a manager with a deep understanding of the technology, someone who can help other engineers master the essential elements of their job. Managers now required technical depth.

Ford also set about recruiting the best graduates of engineering programs worldwide, and developing specific assignments, training, and learning experiences which were aimed at turning them into a highly skilled engineer capable of making autonomous and innovative decisions themselves.

These people would make up the soldiers, battalions, and regiments Ford would need to fight the innovation war necessary to carry them into the 21st century as a viable business.

In sum, Ford built a culture to drive excellence and relentless, continuous improvement. We take a deeper look into the People component of Innovation in Part 4: *Looking Inward: What It Takes to Be a Future Innovator.*

Process

Morgan also worked to eliminate waste, bureaucracy, and maximize value in the product development process itself. Product development processes are highly knowledge driven. Reusable knowledge or knowledge that another person may apply to a similar situation wasn't being captured in an effective manner. Ford began to use (plan–do–check–act, or plan–do–check–adjust) (PDCA) cycles to close any gaps and standardize processes. The result was a new Ford Global Product Development Process.

We take a look at the processes and frameworks that drive the most successfully innovative companies in Chapter 14, Capability: How Innovation Wars Are Managed.

Tools and Technology

What use is all the knowledge in the world if you can't easily access it? Ford, under Morgan's efforts, employed CAD/CAE tools to allow all useful information to be available right when designers needed it. This made it easier to create reliable models and simulations and to standardize problem location and solution. Standardization became the norm.

A single car has about 30,000 parts. That's a lot that can go wrong. Developing standard solutions to most problems enabled designers to focus innovation on the specific areas that make a particular car distinct: fuel economy, value for money, luxury, or style. It also heavily reduced problems later in development and production.

The end result of the changes at the Ford Motor Company in five years was dramatic. $8 billion profit. A two-year market share increase. A $17 stock price. A stronger global supply base. A culture of "One Ford." Thousands of new hires. The Ford Motor Company had done the impossible and dug itself out of looming bankruptcy, not by one magic bullet or killer product, but by incremental innovation that focused on its assets—towering technical competence and product-led innovation.

Yes, you *can* teach an old dog new tricks.

McDonald's: A History of Innovation

It's 1954. A fifty-two-year-old milkshake machine salesman visits his clients at a hamburger restaurant in San Bernardino, California. But he isn't thinking directly about milkshake machine sales. His name is Ray Kroc, and his clients are Dick and Mac McDonald.

Kroc is thinking about the small chain of franchises that recently purchased five multi-mix milkshake machines from him—one for each of their stores. He is thinking about their operation: a small menu of simple items, cheaply priced, their assembly-line "Speedee Service System" for hamburger preparation, and their consistent approach to all aspects of their business. They are bringing efficiency to what has been up to now a fairly slapdash industry.

He is thinking about a vast chain spread across the United States, perhaps the world. Something far more ambitious that what the McDonalds brothers have ever considered. Does he really need this restaurant? Could he do this with any burger joint, or simply create his own? He once worked for room and board at a restaurant in the Midwest simply to learn the business. Does he need this one, he asks himself again?

The McDonald brothers serve much the same kinds of food as hundreds of other similar American restaurants. What this particular chain offers is innovation to the fast food business, by asking what added value they can give the customer. It's this innovation that sets the McDonald brothers' chain apart. Yes, Kroc knows it's *this* chain he wants.

He just doesn't need the McDonald brothers.

"That night in my motel room I did a lot of heavy thinking about what I'd seen during the day," he said. "Visions of McDonald's restaurants dotting crossroads all over the country paraded through my brain."

Over 40 years earlier, Henry Ford brought innovation to the car industry by combining quality car parts with an efficient assembly line process. Ray Kroc did exactly the same thing. Just with burgers. He invented nothing new. He took a good existing concept and made it better.

He began by signing on to sell franchises. The original deal involved Kroc getting 1.9 percent of gross sales from franchises, and of that the McDonalds would get 0.5 percent. Things turned sour in 1961 after the McDonalds signed an agreement to sell the business to Kroc for two million dollars. Some say the McDonalds were cheated out of a verbal promise to receive a share of royalties, but nothing was written down. A nod is as good as a wink. Kroc himself may have been an innovative genius, but his business morals possibly needed improvement.

"If any of my competitors were drowning, I'd stick a hose in their mouth and turn on the water," he said.

Ethics aside, Kroc's empire marched on. He devised unheard-of and exacting specifications for the burger patties that McDonald's restaurants were to serve: "fat content: below 19 percent; weight: 1.6 ounces; diameter: 3.875 inches; onions: 1/4 ounce." The innovative thinking didn't stop there. By the late 1950s, Kroc had constructed McDonald's first food laboratory in Chicago. Its initial mission: to devise a method for making the perfect fried potato. Also unheard of in the fast-food industry.

Yet innovative behavior was an ingrained element in McDonald's culture before Ray Kroc came along, and it would remain so even after his departure and death. Key to this was that the company's management molded an environment in which innovative thinking could occur and prosper and ideas could flow unfettered through the organization.

Sure, franchise holders had very strict rules of what they could serve, how they could serve it, and even who they could buy supplies from, but this regime of extreme conformity applied to process and product—not to ideas. Kroc knew too that markets can change, and that local markets can have subtly different needs. The creative results of this freedom are astonishing when you begin listing them. The Big Mac, Ronald McDonald, Filet-o-Fish, Drive-Thrus and Playlands—all innovations developed by franchisees, then taken on by the McDonald's Corporation. A good idea is a good idea no matter who comes up with it.

Many innovations were more than great product line additions, but actually opened up entirely new areas of business. For example, the creation of a simple product—the Egg McMuffin in 1971—enabled McDonald's to cater for an entire new market: the breakfast customer.

Innovation permeated everything, including the franchise model. Franchising had existed in the fast food and other industries well before McDonald's came along, and usually consisted of the parent company doing everything it could to fleece the franchisers of their earnings. Kroc realized this wasn't a model for long-term growth. Instead he conceived McDonald's as an equal partnership, a balanced triad between McDonald's franchisees, suppliers and employees. This enabled franchisees room to innovate, even within a rigid system.

Today McDonald's has its own innovation center. Located in a nondescript warehouse in Romeoville, Illinois, not far from McDonald's corporate headquarters, the center has one goal: to improve service at the 34,000 McDonald's outlets around the world. Everything gets tested here, from equipment to food, to drive-thru technology to fragrances for the foyer. Nothing is off limits. There's even a full mock-up restaurant where staff from all over the globe come to experiment and learn.

The innovation center is an admission that a company that began doing business in 1955 is now in a very different landscape. Values have changed dramatically, as have consumer attitudes, especially those to do with nutrition and the environment. The impact of the Information Era is that customers have a lot more data easily at their fingertips. The appearance in the 2000s of detailed nutritional information on packaging was a coup for consumers who sought to drive company action. Some other recent changes that show McDonald's acute awareness of market unpredictability include:

- Promising to source white fish from sustainable fisheries
- Only sourcing chicken farmed without antibiotics
- Committing to a target for purchase of verified sustainable beef

What's next? Well, *McDonald's Next*—a re-developed version of the brand that opened in Hong Kong in 2016 and promises to be "modern and progressive." No more traditional red-and-yellow color scheme and harsh light—that's all replaced by ambient lighting, glass and shiny metal interiors, and (gasp!) a full-service salad bar. The McDonald's Next salad bar is filled with around twenty ingredients including choices of salad base greens, plus different cheese varieties, three flavors of sauces, quinoa—all designed for the customer to mix and match.

McDonald's Next also offers table service after six p.m., along with premium coffee blends. Society is changing, customers' needs are changing, and McDonald's knows it. The biggest lesson of McDonald's is to keep in touch with your customers and keep evolving. "A laurel rested upon quickly wilts" was a favorite of Kroc's sayings, and this attitude became ingrained in the company's culture.

The McDonald's of today is a very different beast than when it began, but it didn't change path overnight. It was a slow process that involved incremental change upon incremental change—with just one possible exception: the McDonald brothers actually set up their first restaurant to sell hickory-smoked BBQ items, but switched very quickly when burgers became menu best sellers.

As we look back at historically successful companies, we can see that the ones that embraced change and innovation, like Ford and McDonald's have survived. While the world may look very different than it did when Ford and McDonald's were "startups," the same principles apply. Embracing change, adapting to the constantly evolving needs of the consumer, and taking risks are still critical for a business to thrive. As they say, the more things change, the more they stay the same.

Chapter 3

WHAT WE CAN LEARN FROM THE LEGENDS AND FAILURES OF INNOVATION

W hy exactly is innovation so important? Although a popular current buzzword, the business world has a long history of innovation. In fact, innovation is an intrinsic element in remaining viable as a business; those businesses that have innovated have survived, and those that haven't have perished. Innovation is important because it improves the status quo and makes life better. Innovation increases productivity, aids in the development of new products and services, and drives higher profits, job creation, and income growth.

Quite simply, innovation is the best way to sustain economic prosperity.

There's a distinction to recognize, however: innovation exists with a big "I" and small "i". We've talked of both. Both have proved historically vital to business success. "Innovation" consists of truly revolutionary inventions like the car, the bar code, and the internet. But "innovation" also includes small incremental evolutionary improvements to existing products. The cellphone. The modern car. The iPod.

According to a 2015 study by IBM of more than 5,000 executives in over seventy countries, nearly 60 percent of CEOs now value the pursuit of truly disruptive innovation over mere incremental improvement in their businesses. Corporate self-awareness and realization of their own limitations means Heads of Innovation are looking to partners to help evolve into innovative cultures and test new ground.

We began discussing Apple, so let's return to the man perhaps most closely associated with innovation for the past thirty years: Steve Jobs. Jobs was acutely aware of the importance innovative behavior plays in business. When he returned to Apple after a twelve-year absence in 1997, Apple was close to bankruptcy. "The cure for Apple is not cost-cutting," Jobs said. "The cure for Apple is to innovate its way out of its current predicament." Under Jobs' leadership Apple began to launch one innovation after another after another—iMac, iPod, iTunes, iPhone, and iPad—revolutionizing the computer, entertainment, music, retail, mobile, and telecommunications industries.

When Jobs was (often) asked to discuss how to be innovative—his answer was characteristically direct. You don't need Lego strewn across the campus for creative brainstorming or stale team-building activities. "It's like someone who's not cool pretending to be cool. It's painful to watch."

What made Jobs and his historical business-world predecessors' innovators? While all were individuals of their eras, and no doubt had unique skill sets, there are certain characteristics and principles that tend to guide people as innovators and set them apart from the rest. Successful entrepreneurs who realized the importance of innovation—people like Henry Ford, Ingvar Kamprad, Bill Gates, Steve Jobs, and Larry Page—would all likely fit to (and agree with) these principles of what it takes to be an innovative genius. That is not to say that every successful entrepreneur or innovator possesses every quality on this list—but most of them possess many of these characteristics.

1. **Passion.** When once asked what advice he would give a young entrepreneur looking for career guidance, Steve Jobs said: "Go out and a get a job as a busboy or something until you find something you're really passionate about." Jobs was not per se passionate about computers; he

was passionate about creating a company that could build tools to help people unleash their passion. Passion is everything. Innovation won't happen without it. Innovation requires a company to collectively surmount numerous obstacles—financial, cultural, psychological—and the "activation energy" to surmount those obstacle requires passion.

2. **Vision.** In 1979 when Steve Jobs saw the graphical user interface demonstrated at the Xerox research facility in Palo Alto, California, he knew immediately that this new technology would make computers appealing to "everyday people." His vision was to allow everyday people to make use of a computer. Xerox scientists didn't realize the potential because their "vision" was limited to making copiers. In other words, two people can see the exactly the same thing, but perceive it differently based on their vision.

3. **Leadership.** Innovators lead through building honest relationships with employees and colleagues and tend to value the input of others. **Authentic leaders** are men and women who are aware of their strengths, their weaknesses, and their emotions. They are results driven rather than self-interest driven, and they create trusting, creative environments. CEO Sam Palmisano, who is often credited with reviving IBM's fortunes in the 2000s, is regarded as a culture-focused, authentic leader. In a speech to mark IBM's 100th anniversary in 2011, he said: "The old model of the heroic superman is increasingly archaic. The most active and successful leaders today see themselves as part of the global community and peer groups. They listen as well as they speak. Never confuse charisma with leadership. The first job of a leader is to enable an organization to survive without him or her. The key to that is to build a sustainable culture."

4. **Collaboration.** Nothing happens in a vacuum, least of all innovation. A true innovator is very aware of their weakness so will surround themselves with people who will make up for it. They build and sustain active, vibrant networks of employees, as assets within their organization. Innovators direct from the center of their organizations, empowering and demanding employees to be creative and autonomous. There's a well-loved joke that circles Google's offices, that aptly demonstrates CEO

Larry Page's philosophy to aim for the skies. The joke goes something like this: "A brainiac who works in the lab walks into Page's office one day wielding his latest world-changing invention—a time machine. As the scientist reaches for the power cord to begin a demo, Page fires off the question: 'Why do you need to plug it in?'"

5. **Acceptance of failure.** Innovators are not afraid of going after more complex solutions, even if it means taking higher risks. If you're thinking outside the box, some ideas will naturally fail. Fine. Put that idea aside and move on to the next one. The 1957 Ford Edsel was the biggest automobile marketing disaster of the 20th century. Did Henry Ford sit round like a cry-baby? No, he got back to work, had the scheduled 1960 compact model redesignated the Mercury Comet—which sold quite nicely, actually.

6. **Embracing change.** Innovators understand innovation is not a one-time thing, or something only start-up companies can do well. Along with the hundreds of examples of long-standing company failures, there are also some examples of those that have continuously reached above and beyond what they have done before to stay competitive. McDonald's began selling barbecue spare ribs; IKEA sold pencils.

7. **Mastery of storytelling.** Steve Jobs was the world's greatest corporate storyteller, turning new product launches into something of an art form. It doesn't matter if you have great ideas—if you cannot convince others to take action on those ideas they will never become innovative new products or services. For every idea that turns into a successful innovation, you'll find a few thousand ideas that never gain traction because the people behind those ideas failed to tell a compelling and convincing story for why.

And lastly and most importantly:

8. **Thinking big.** You'll see a small sign plastered on doors at Microsoft's Redmond campus. It reads: "Change the world, or go home." It speaks of the way not only Bill Gates but all innovators live their lives. Microsoft was built around the recognition that software would be a world-changing innovation, one that a whole industry could be built

around. There was no software industry before Microsoft. Microsoft created it. **An innovator is in the world-changing business**. If not, they might as well go home.

The use of the war metaphor in this book about innovation is not meant to be crude or insensitive to the sacrifice and bravery of the people who face the rigors of the battlefield. But it is an intentional and useful one when characterizing the struggle faced by organizations that want to embrace true innovation. Innovation: the *buzzword* may sound sexy, but innovation in *practice* is dirty and difficult; it's like working in the trenches. To possess passion, vision, leadership, to embrace failure and change, to wield the power of story, and to think big—none of these traits are small things on their own, and when taken together, as they must be for an organization to win an innovation war, they are estimable. Innovation is not a simple pursuit; it's a gargantuan operation, the success of which is founded on a holistic identity that's understood and embraced across an entire organization.

Kodak: How Past Success Ensured Future Failure

But this identity, even once established within an organization, can be elusive. It must be constantly cultivated and renewed, or the dreaded complacency seeps in and quickly leads to ruin. Just ask the company that revolutionized and dominated an entire industry—photographic film—for decades.

"Kodachrome
They give us those nice bright colors
They give us the greens of summers
Makes you think all the world's
A sunny day, oh yeah
I got a Nikon camera
I love to take a photograph
So mama, don't take my Kodachrome away"

Lyrics © Paul Simon

Unfortunately, "taken" (into bankruptcy) was exactly the fate of Kodachrome and its manufacturer, Kodak, at the hands of management that could not see future opportunities due to the company's vast past successes. Make no mistake: Kodak's previous success through innovation was monumental. This was a company whose founder, George Eastman, was an innovator through and through. He invented roll film and developed the first film camera. He embraced color film when the rest of the world was still seeing in black and white. In 1996, Kodak was ranked the fourth most valuable brand behind Disney, Coca-Cola, and McDonald's. It employed 140,000 people and controlled 90 percent of the film market.

In 2012, however, Kodak filed for bankruptcy.

So just what happened in those sixteen years?

You could say everything and nothing. Kodak did not fail purely because of the unforeseen onslaught of digital technology. Few people realize today that Kodak *invented* the digital camera in 1975. The corporate response at the time according to Steve Sasson—the Kodak engineer who created it: "that's cute—but don't tell anyone about it." At the time, this reaction may have been excusable, written down as sheer unfamiliarity or inability to recognize the potential in what Sasson's team had created.

But Kodak's unwillingness to innovate itself into renewed relevance continued well beyond the 1970s, becoming less and less excusable as time marched on and the new digital reality became more obvious and unavoidable.

Kodak, like Xerox in the computer market, could have dominated the digital camera market for many years. Although they recognized the threat of digital, they did little about it. Even way back in 1981, the company commissioned an internal study that identified a ten-year window for Kodak to adjust to the looming digital future—but the company failed to use that time to prepare for the massive change ahead. Instead they continued to double down on their traditional film business.

It was 2005 before Kodak was producing digital cameras as serious consumer products—*thirty years after they had invented them.* Kodak was an old company, having been founded in 1888. Its longevity and its long-dominant position in the photographic film industry had created a deep-seated complacency throughout the organization, one that was blinding it to the challenges of the future.

The late '80s saw another series of crucial missteps. In 1988, Kodak spent $5 billion to buy a medical chemical company, Sterling Drug Inc. of New York—on the rationale that film also used chemicals. They soon found it wasn't really the same thing, and the new acquisition was eventually sold at a huge loss.

The following year, 1989, was another critical year. A long-serving CEO was about to retire. Phil Samper and Kay R. Whitmore were the candidates to be the next CEO. The former represented a break with tradition, someone who understood the future and wanted to take Kodak in the direction of digital. The later represented the tried and true traditional film business. The board elected Whitmore.

They attempted a hybrid camera utilizing digital technology to preview pictures, which still used film. Customers just asked, "why?" In later years as losses mounted, they began producing printers and digital photo software. Customers just weren't buying it. Literally.

All the time Kodak had staff within the organization who did understand the future of the camera market, and had creative and innovative ideas about what could be done to combat Kodak's woes. Management never listened to them. One example was Kodak Information Management Systems (KIMS), a big internal project aimed at eliminating media like paper and microfilm in order to create a "paperless office." But KIMS never took off because upper management just couldn't give up on their commitment to film. Potential KIMS customers saw this indecision and stayed away.

Stifled by management that couldn't see the potential in the burgeoning digital revolution, many of Kodak's employees, Phil Samper included, took their ideas to other companies that could see the future. Kay Whitmore lasted only three years at the helm of Kodak before being ousted by the company's board in 1993.

In January 2012, under its third CEO since Whitmore's departure, Kodak filed for Chapter 11 bankruptcy protection, its stock closing at $0.36 a share that day.

What lessons can be learned from the cataclysmic failure of Kodak? Here are a few, adapted from some of the insights in Vincent Barabba's book *The Decision Loom: A Design for Interactive Decision-Making in Organizations*:

1. **An organization must have a culture that is open to change from the top down.** Founder George Eastman was open and adopted disruptive new technology (color film when black and white was the norm); something his successors were unable to do.

2. **Management must be able to see the organization holistically.** Kodak, like Xerox, had little appreciation of just how important the technology being created in their own labs really was. They were unable to see the potential of the technology to transform the business and take it into the future.

3. **Listen to what your customers want.** One of Kodak's earliest slogans was "You press the button—we'll do the rest." Digital cameras offered consumers just this. Rather than sell the benefit (easy photography) Kodak kept selling the product (physical film).

4. **Make decisions interactively, using all the vast knowledge available within the company**. Kodak had people who knew what to do. No one listened to them. Sound familiar?

Kodak had the technology, and it had the talent. It certainly had the legacy of innovation. Arguably, the company had what it needed to win an innovation war, in spades—but it lacked the organizational culture and foresight to put those pieces together. The cultural inertia—the comfort created by its past success through innovation—was just too great. Although for a long period of its history Kodak was able to put these "innovation inputs" to work, its example demonstrates how challenging it is to sustain an innovative mindset across an entire organization.

When you look at Kodak management as a whole during this period of decline, they exhibited strikingly few of the eight characteristics of innovative leaders we discussed earlier in the chapter. At the doorstep of the digital revolution, with much of the raw material they needed to succeed in this new era in their very hands, Kodak leadership lacked the passion and vision that would have allowed them to think big. Adherence to a tried-and-true business model created a distinct resistance to embracing change. As a result, Kodak's leaders were unable to foster the kind of multi-level collaboration that would help the company innovate into the new era. Instead, that new era dragged Kodak forward, kicking and screaming, until the company was forced to admit defeat.

Chapter 4

STAGNATION, DECAY, AND
THE EMBERS OF WAR

A s we come to the end of the first section of this book, we find
ourselves at a crossroads. At this crossroads is the intersection of two
key elements. One is the acceleration of the rate of change across
multiple industries, spurred by the growing digital reality. This acceleration of
change has resulted in two things: a reduction in the longevity of companies
and products—of the "shelf lives" of both corporations and the things they sell.
By the same token, this acceleration has also driven a marked increase in how
quickly previously unknown competitors can become dominant forces in their
respective markets.

The second thing we find at this intersection is the set of forces and conditions
that are preventing incumbents from accelerating in this new world. These are
the structural realities of many big organizations these days, based on hierarchical
forms of management and decision-making that are simply not nimble enough.
Large organizations have much to learn from the startup model, as we'll explore
in Chapter 7, but it's not enough just to observe and emulate—to truly innovate,
organizations first need to become self-aware.

Stagnation on the Battlefield and the Storefront

In most large organizations, the key decision makers are a world away from the end customer, often five or six tiers apart. As a result, they simply can't empathize with their customer in a way that would allow them to drive effective prioritization and investment decisions. What they end up driving, in a sense, is stagnation. These decision makers are stuck in a world where they do not really understand their market, disconnected from a sense of priority about what they should be building for their customers.

We see these stagnation-inducing forces on the delivery side of many big companies, as well, where the approach to building products and services is still stuck the industrial era—products and services make it to market months and years after they're prioritized. In the startup world, of course, delivery happens over the course of days and weeks. This world is agile, iterative, able to respond to the market in nearly real time.

In sum, we are looking at two very different structural approaches to the competitive landscape, and the tension that results when they clash. When Uber and Airbnb first started, they were easily dismissed in their respective markets. But both companies snuck up to their competitors, and leapfrogged them to become the largest players in their respective markets.

How did they do this? Quite simply, by valuing and applying to their business metrics that traditional players weren't even thinking about. Traditional hotels look at certain measures related to revenue and performance; Airbnb used a completely different metric. They leveraged the power of deep analytics linked to a qualitative understanding of their key ecosystem player—the Airbnb hosts. The company's priorities focused on creating "successful" hosts, using the words the hosts themselves used to describe success.

And so it went with the death of Kodak. The company that invented the digital camera had always focused on one key metric above all: quality. For Kodak, quality was the be-all, end-all when it came to photography. And they made business decisions according to the assumption that consumers would value this criterion as much as the company did. In reality, however, quality was not the key metric for Kodak's customers. That metric? Convenience. These customers were looking for an easy way to create and share images. Convenience was the killer benefit, the key metric toward which Kodak should have innovated. But it didn't.

As outsiders with the benefit of foresight, it's easy to wonder why Kodak failed to recognize this basic truth. But stagnation and inertia—especially when it's based on immense past success—can be blinding, and it was for Kodak's management.

It's easy to think that military organizations are inherently wired for agility in decision-making, but the truth is less forgiving in this arena, too. In the early years of the conflict in Afghanistan, the US military was handcuffed by the reality of their decision-making structure. Troops on the ground were forced to seek approval for many decisions all the way up the chain to Washington via multiple layers of hierarchy in order to make decisions on the ground. Soldiers would find themselves in the middle of a market in Kabul, not entrusted to decide whether to arrest, kill, or feed the person in front of them, because they had to wait for orders from Washington.

But once the battle shifted to the mountains, this approach became completely untenable. The military was forced to change tack. Commanders realized that what they needed to do was allow teams on the ground to make their own decisions independent of their hierarchical roles. In this way, the military in Afghanistan became more of a distributed organization, one that empowered its people on the ground to make decisions as needed in the context of the moment and their environment.

Back on the corporate side, we can look for insights at the demise of another once-great US retailer: Toys 'R Us. For many large retailers, 2017 was the year of bankruptcies. At least 27 large retailers filed for bankruptcy protection in 2017, including RadioShack, Payless ShoeSource, Gymboree, Vitamin World, and yes, Toys 'R Us. These companies all failed to adapt, in one way or another, to the new competitive landscape and the pressures it has brought.

In the case of Toys 'R Us, we're talking about a business with a product niche that should never go out of style: toys. Despite having a product set everyone wants to buy, Toys 'R Us failed to realize that this wasn't enough—that they needed to innovate if they wanted to compete with Amazon, primarily. For Toys 'R Us—and many companies today—attempting to compete merely on product and price simply won't work; Amazon will beat you day in and day out. They're more agile, have better distribution, and offer a better customer experience thanks to their recommendation engine, review system, and customer-first philosophy.

So what happened to Toys 'R Us? They failed to realize that their biggest structural constraint—their physical retail locations—should have been turned into a differentiator. Instead, it became a hindrance.

Companies that insist on staying "physical" in this day and age need to offer a compelling reason for customers to want to walk into their stores. If you know you want an Avengers action figure, you already know what you want, and you know you can find it quickly on Amazon. Because of the web, fewer and fewer people today are entering the buying process without already knowing what they want. They know what they want—and they know they can get it cheaply and conveniently somewhere like Amazon. So why would they want to spend time traveling to a Toys 'R Us store to get that Avengers doll?

Toys 'R Us should have realized early on that if they wanted to peg themselves to physical retail, they needed to change the physical retail experience. Instead of a big box store, make it a playground. As Gary Vaynerchuk said in a 2017 YouTube video, [Toys 'R Us] could be killing it with their locations… but they choose to just sell toys out of it."

The irony is that all the way back in 2000, Toys 'R Us turned to Amazon to do a lot of their fulfillment. They *saw* the promise of the Internet in transforming retail—but they didn't *embrace* that promise. Initially, the deal was a boon for both sides, making Toys 'R Us more competitive and giving Amazon's toy inventory a much-needed boost. But over time Amazon brokered partnerships with several of Toys 'R Us's competitors, while simultaneously drawing customers away from Toys 'R Us own website.

Over the course of the next decade and a half, Amazon turned into the behemoth it has become, while Toys 'R Us began to languish. Toys 'R Us had put too many of their eggs in Amazon's basket, trusting another company to innovate them into the 21st century. And at the same time, they neglected to see how they might transform their retail legacy into an innovation opportunity.

As Vaynerchuk said in that YouTube video, "[Toys 'R Us] didn't innovate. And when you don't innovate, you die."

Self-Awareness and the Embers of War

That brings us back to the metaphor on which this book is based, of a war of innovation. In one sense, this war is akin to the traditional concept of a "land grab", although in our case what is being sought is the customer dollar. But the war exists on many fronts, both internal and external. It's a war against competitors, both direct and indirect; against established foes and disruptors just entering your space. It's also a war against stagnation and decay, of the entropy that occurs when innovation isn't fueled from within.

And the "embers" of war: Are these the embers of a dying fire—or one that's about to come to life? I leave this question intentionally open-ended, because the challenge for companies in this day and age is to pose this question, and answer it for themselves: "Are we starting the fire, or is it dying?"

I choose not to attempt to answer this question because what's needed more than anything right now for large companies that want to win the innovation war is *self-awareness*. Cultivating the self-awareness that can lead to organizational agility and adaptability is the biggest challenge for large organizations today. Different industries and companies exist in many different states and stages, and each one needs to do its own work to understand the state and stage of their own industry and company.

A basic strengths, weakness, opportunities, and threats (SWOT) analysis is one way for incumbent companies to get a better view of their internal and external realities, and understand what *their* innovation war may look like. What are you good at? What are you failing at? What opportunities are out there, waiting to be tapped? And what's standing in the way?

But before any such analysis can happen, the primary question to

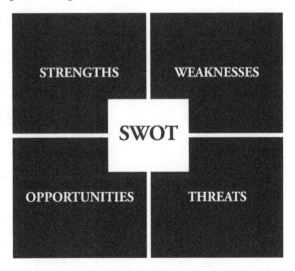

answer is this: Are you willing to do the work of self-reflection at an organizational level? In a world of accelerated change and new structural realities, this is the first and deepest shift that large companies will need to embrace if they want to have a fighting chance in their own war of innovation. And to embrace all of the opportunities that exist in this changing landscape.

PART 2

LOOKING OUTWARD: HOW INNOVATION IS DRIVING CHANGE TODAY

Chapter 5

DYING INDUSTRIES AND OTHER TARGET-RICH ENVIRONMENTS

W hat does the future hold? The reality is any company in the Fortune 500 that is older than ten years is now ripe for disruption. According to the Olin School of Business, 40 percent of today's Fortune 500 companies will be gone in the next ten years.

Disruptive innovation, as coined by Clayton Christensen, describes a process by which a product or service takes root in simple applications at the bottom end of the market and moves obstinately up market tiers, eventually dislodging long-established companies.

Large companies focus on the high end of the market and sustaining innovation, by upgrading product offerings with new features to bring in higher-paying customers, while subsequently ignoring everyday mid-market consumers who just want simple low-cost products. In comes a smaller company with a basic offering. The larger company still focuses on the top end of the market, offering still more bells and whistles that fewer and fewer people want to pay for. Meanwhile, the disruptor changes the performance benchmark for its product offering to appeal to more people and continues to grow. By the time the large company notices, the disruptor has begun to take over the market.

The larger and more entrenched an industry is, the greater the chance of disruption. Many of the companies serving these industries are bogged down with bureaucracies, and inflexible processes and procedures. Nimble, responsive and innovative won't work in such environments, and as a result the customer always comes last. But this shouldn't be the case. Truly great innovators co-create new products and services with the market, by constantly re-asking fundamental questions about what the customer values.

We live in an era of change. Nothing is static. It's the age of disruption. Whole industries will change. Some companies will fall. Others will become even stronger. New ones will appear. Although it might seem like the biggest markets have already undergone change, there are still hordes of $10 billion-plus industries that are underserved or have been doing things the same old way for decades. Of those, some of the sectors most vulnerable to future disruptive innovation include:

- Agriculture
- Banking
- Construction
- Credit reporting
- Data informatics
- Education
- Enterprise Computing
- Finance
- Groceries
- Ready-to-Eat Meals
- Healthcare
- Human Resources
- Insurance
- Legal
- Military Industry
- News

- Online Dating
- Packaging
- Shipping
- Sports Gaming
- Talent Management
- Travel
- Wine

Let's look at a few of these examples in more detail.

Education: Massively Open to Disruption

Universities and higher learning organizations are surely some of the most old-school (no pun intended), entrenched institutions you'll find anywhere on the planet. Tuition fees increase each year. Student loans are huge. The largest and most elite universities act more like financial institutions than educators. Lecturers teach in closed formats to roughly thirty students, as they always have. There is limited use of technology to transfer information in a more economical or efficient way. As a result, it's difficult to imagine that traditional education institutions could reinvent themselves in a more user-centric way.

That's where disruptive innovators might come into play—and some might say they are already with us. One example that's on the rise is Massive Open Online Courses (MOOCs). Online companies like Coursera are flipping the value proposition of established educational institutions. Previously, the value of universities and other traditional colleges lay primarily in the *delivery of educational content*, but content can be consumed anytime, and via a multitude of technologies. Instead, an educational institution that wants to thrive in the new reality needs to pivot to the *application* of learning—something we'll get to in a minute.

Coursera partners with universities and other education providers to make courses freely available online in an array of subjects, including Humanities, Social Sciences, Medicine, Biology, Business, Computer Science, Mathematics, and Digital Marketing. Each course provides short video lectures and access to peer learning groups—with students delivering weekly assignments and regular tests and exams.

Using new technology, Coursera moves away from the previously held belief that for learning to occur, educator and student need to be in the same place. Cheating? Proof identity? Technology is already providing answers to these and other long standing roadblocks to distance-learning. For example, during tests and quizzes, Coursera's box of tech tricks includes an analysis of keystroke dynamics during typing—in combination with webcam identity verification to confirm the identity of students.

You can't totally claim the big boys of education aren't trying, though. Even established institutions are dipping their toes in the uncharted waters MOOCs have been exploring. EdX is one example, a platform that resulted from a partnership between Harvard and MIT in 2012. This non-profit organization offers a wide range of university-level courses online—many of which are free. It also conducts extensive research into how students use its services in this learning environment.

Can MOOCs replace face-to-face classes in facilitating learning? Very possibly. The problem is that the value of Ivy League schooling is less about the quality of education offered and more in the prestige associated with these institutions, which has a lot to do with their exclusivity. The entry criteria is ultra-hard. Few get into Harvard, Yale, Princeton, and Brown, all of which admitted fewer than 10 percent of applicants in 2017. This exclusivity is unlikely to change significantly in the near future. As such, you'll be disappointed if you think Harvard Business School is about to start offering degrees to everyone, online, anytime soon. What MOOCs don't offer are official college degrees— you know, the kind that can help land you a job, and that, strangely enough, are mostly what college students are paying for.

Until now, education was about content *delivery inside* the classroom and *application outside* the classroom. We're seeing now how Coursera and other online platforms are flipping that paradigm. You absorb the content through video and other online learning and spend the time with professors applying the content, so the universities that have understood that are thriving in the flipped economy.

Ten years ago, e-learning was a huge element in corporate educational programs. If you were a multinational corporation involved in the training of your staff then e-learning was a more saleable way. Today in many cases, instead of engaging e-learning, companies are saying to staff: "Here's $1,000. Here's Coursera. Here's what you need to learn." Staff can take the course, and expense it when they pass. It's a great way of building competency over time. The rise of MOOCs also means that staff can easily pursue education outside their current profession, which gives them a key advantage in the marketplace should they ever want to make a career shift.

What will happen over time is that more educational content will slowly become free to access. You don't have to look too far on YouTube to find millions of people all over the world willing to teach you any topic you might want to learn. Want to learn German? Algebra? Advanced calculus? There are YouTube video courses for all three. The differentiation that is yet to emerge will be in the recognition of the successful application of that content: Once you've learned the content, how do you demonstrate you can apply it?

A good example of this is what happens in Silicon Valley. Fewer people are going to business school or tech school to learn the tools of the trade. Instead, they go online, to forums or Code Academy or Udacity to learn new computer languages so they can build their startup. Very few startup founders are amazing tech geniuses who are light years ahead of anybody else on the planet. They just make sure they learn the skills and tools appropriate for their context. A founder who doesn't know how to code but needs to build a prototype of their killer app will go online and hack it out for five days to learn Ruby on Rails 101. They learn what they need to, as they need to, so they can build their products. This is a model of skill development called **just-in-time learning**, where you focus on learning the exact skills you need to succeed at a specific task or meet a specific goal. And it's a big part of the future of learning.

Two current buzzwords in education are "blended learning" and "flipped classrooms," and both refer to a combination of online content along with a reorganization of the traditional lecture-then-exam teaching format. However, free online courses aren't going to revolutionize education until there is a corresponding scheme of free or low-fee qualifications, one not controlled by traditional colleges, but that is still broadly accepted by employers, and can thus help open new employment opportunities to. Only when that happens will the economic foundations beneath universities really begin to worry.

The good news is technological innovators are working on that, too. New information technology could be poised to transform the established college degree. Along has come the Mozilla Foundation, the company that originally brought the world the Firefox web browser, which has spent the last few years creating the **Open Badges project**. "Badges" are electronic qualifications that are issued through any credible organization or collegiate. Badges indicate specific skills and knowledge, and are backed up by digital evidence of how and why, exactly, the badge was earned.

The system is based on an open standard, so students/learners can pool multiple badges from different education providers to tell the full story of their achievements—both online and off. It's an answer to the traditional approach of being tied down to one place, to study one course at one institution. Isn't it a little antiquated, that in the on-demand age, when millennials are turning their backs on television to demand entertainment where and when they want it, that as students they're expected to spend three to ten years of their life in one city, at one university, studying the same course in order to get the qualification they want?

The promise of the Digital Badges project is that it'll be possible to study where you want, gain recognized qualifications, and display your authenticated skills and achievements on social networking profiles, job sites, and other websites.

In this way, education could become truly "open source," out of the hands of the establishment and back in the hands of the consumer.

Insurance: From Pools to People

Nothing is sure to put people to sleep more quickly than talking about insurance (perhaps accounting). Start talking about insurance to venture capital investors and they'll begin to slowly put away their wallets. It's not a sexy industry like travel or technology and perhaps that's one small reason why it's been resistant to disruptive innovation.

But here's a sexy idea to keep you interested. You've heard of peer-to-peer file sharing, and peer-to-peer reviews are an important part of models like Uber and Airbnb—so what about peer-to-peer insurance?

It's not exactly a new idea. Peer-to-peer was, in fact, the original model of the insurance world. Mutual insurance companies were formed initially by farmers, and by company and home owners, to protect against fires as a way to share their losses and gains around. (A *mutual insurance* company is one owned entirely by its policyholders.) It's a peer-to-peer model because individuals join together to insure against a risk and diversify that risk amongst the group, rather than having one person transfer the risk to another, which is how most traditional insurance business models work today.

And there are websites today setting up business models where you can do just this. The aim of peer-to-peer insurance is to make insurance more affordable and to give individuals more control. For this to work, a group of "policyholders" join together online. If a claim occurs they then support each other financially. There are different models. A portion of the insurance premiums paid may go into a group fund, and the rest to a traditional insurer. Minor policyholders' claims can be first paid out of the group fund. For larger claims, the regular insurer may be called upon. If there are no claims over a period of a year, then the insurance premiums are reduced for the group, or the policyholder may get their share refunded from the group pool or credited toward the next policy year.

One example of an up-and-coming online peer-to-peer insurance providers is the European-based Friendsurance. Friendsurance's service is based on a **shareconomy approach,** where policy owners who desire the same insurance type form new groups or join an existing community. A group is akin to a Facebook-like social network. All that's necessary for it to function is that all members of each group/community share the same type of insurance, i.e. liability, household contents, earthquake, or auto insurance.

"But hold on a moment," you might say. "Aren't there rules to prevent people from forming their own insurance companies?" Well, yes, of course; there are regulations all over the show. But tell that to Uber, which found taxi industry regulation could only stand in the way for so long.

The centuries-old insurance sector is just a collective "pooling" of the world's risk—large, generalized "buckets" of risk based on broad categorizations of people. But now that we are all connected, and so much data is available on each of us as individuals, this pooling is less valuable. Insurance is still largely an industry that thinks about premium and loss ratios using a thirty-year-old view on risk avoidance. But with connected, real-time technologies, the ability to create real-time risk mitigation services means the gross risk of a pool is significantly reduced by leveraging end-user intent and behavioral patterns. In today's world, with incredible access to rich, individualized data, there's no reason insurance companies' models can't manage risk at the individual policyholder level in real time. What did you do today? How many steps did you take? What did you eat? What did you expose yourself to environmentally? These are data points that are available to the insurance company to conduct a personalized risk assessment and customize your policy accordingly.

Insurance companies can also utilize targeted interventions to reduce risky behaviors, and allow you to reap the benefits in terms of lower premiums. Today some automotive insurance companies will offer you a discount if you allow them to install a sensor in your car that reports key factors like speed and acceleration—basically all the data they need to tell if you're a good or bad driver.

Is the same possible for your body? It sure is. Want cheap health or life insurance? Then how about the idea of letting an insurance company monitor your health by sequencing your genome? Or imagine sensors that help you avoid risk factors for allergies, or cancer. This can all be done with technology right now.

Luckily, there are also protections in place so that you can't be denied insurance or charged a higher rate if your tests come back less than positive. The Genetic Information Nondiscrimination Act of 2008 (GINA) is a US federal law that makes "genetic discrimination" illegal in health insurance and employment. Genetic discrimination is a newly devised term that means "the misuse of genetic information." So companies can't discriminate against you based on genetics— but you could be given a discount if you can show you're living a healthy lifestyle and also genetically predisposed against certain conditions.

That's health insurance. But there are other scenarios, potentially right around the corner, that could see the collapse of other segments of today's traditional insurance industry.

As autonomous (driverless, self-driving, robotic) cars begin to appear on the roads, there may be no more need for auto insurance. Autonomous cars are programmed not to crash, so why insure them? Another terrifying future scenario for the insurance industry is that people may stop buying cars altogether. The future of car ownership could end up looking a lot like to the computer server business model today. Most companies no longer own their IT servers; instead, they use cloud-based servers from companies such as Google and Amazon. Cars could go the same way, with companies and individuals renting access to autonomous vehicles from Google or another provider. If you don't own a car, and they don't crash, there's not much for you to insure.

This kind of technological innovation threatens to bring obsolescence to many areas of traditional insurance.

Healthcare: From Intuitive to Precise

"Hand out a pill or cut it out" has for the better part of a century been the mantra of Western medicine. Western medicine is based on episodic diagnosis and treatment. Each episode is treated in isolation, mainly to protect the physician from liability.

Healthcare is another industry sheltered by regulation. As a result, little in the way of innovative change in the healthcare business model has occurred over the past two decades. Although disruptive innovation has brought reduced costs and accessibility to customers in a variety of industries, health care remains expensive and inaccessible to many.

Current thinking tends to ask how we can afford healthcare, when that should be flipped to ask how we can make healthcare affordable. There are plenty of parallels. Other products and services that were once highly priced, kept to the realms of exclusive users in large organizations requiring operatives who had extensive technical training, are now widely available and affordable to the consumer. Computers, for example once existed only in exclusive research institutions. Healthcare is very similar.

Healthcare comprises professional operatives (doctors) who have extensive, lengthy and costly training. Access to the services is limited (by cost) just as computers in a research environment were once restricted. So why is it that computers and other products and services that used to be expensive are now cheap and freely available?

Disruptive innovation, which comprises three elements:

1. **Technology** that simplifies, standardizes, and builds solutions.
2. **Business models** that deliver simple solutions affordably, accessibly, and profitably.
3. **A value network** of businesses that support each other and form the infrastructure.

Can something similar to what's happened in other industries happen in healthcare? Absolutely.

For one, technological advances aren't exactly lacking. Healthcare has a strong high-tech support industry that is rich with new discoveries each year. Yet despite such sophisticated medical technologies, health care has not yet been disrupted to any significant degree. The reason is that technology has most often been implemented within the traditional business model—that is, it's used to help hospitals and doctors solve problems, become more efficient, and make more profits, and not necessarily to make care more affordable or accessible to customers. New technology simply "slots into" the system while making little change to it.

In *The Innovator's Prescription*, Clayton Christensen argues that disruption in the healthcare industry will come "through new business models, technologies, and value networks," and that attention to business models is the first indispensable step to health care reform.

Remember that although initially a disruptive product or service is not as good as similar existing products or services, it is still good enough for many customers, it costs less than the incumbent's offering, and it improves over time.

It's hard not to see the potential for disruptive innovation in healthcare. Americans spent $2.9 trillion in this area in 2013. Obamacare was a good start, but the U.S. healthcare industry is still in crisis. How many consumers can be said to be truly happy at with the services they receive? Two huge challenges stand out: large, monopolistic institutions, and mountains of regulation. As a US healthcare consumer, you still face stacks of paper forms to fill out again and again, along with often long waits—and just try getting a second opinion or a referral! Breakthroughs occur every week in science and biotech, but it still seems impossible to leverage this success into better service for consumers.

The traditional healthcare fee-for-service business model dates from the 19th century, long before technology such as diagnostic imaging and biochemical testing became matters of routine. Traditional intuitive medicine, which depends on a physician's experience and ability to recognize configurations of symptoms in individual patients, is just as anachronistic as the business model it serves.

According to Christensen, "Significant improvement will come only through the creation of fundamentally focused business models that … are highly disruptive to the present profit formulas of general hospitals."

But there are emerging trends that suggest the potential for true innovative disruption in healthcare.

Technology-based "precision medicine" is a developing methodology for disease treatment and prevention that takes into account individual differences in lifestyle, genes, and environment, for each individual. The rise of (and reduction in costs of) genome sequencing has made it possible to classify people into subpopulations of "interest" for certain diseases. It enables practitioners to focus on prevention and treatment among populations who will benefit, while excluding unnecessary spending, treatment, and side-effects for those that won't. In this way, precision medicine could eventually replace or reduce the need for intuitive medicine.

In addition, new business models in which doctors delegate routine work to lesser-paid technicians have the potential to create savings for the entire industry. Medical practitioners have until now maintained a "hands-on" approach, precisely because they benefit financially when they do the work themselves. But today the technology exists for less-costly technicians to perform aspects of the work typically performed by doctors, particularly in the diagnostic arena.

Incumbents and would-be innovators would both do well to take note: It is precisely in those industries, like healthcare and insurance—industries in which "business as usual" has been "usual" for so long that disruption seems impossible—where we are likely to see innovation take off in the next five to ten years.

Chapter 6

THE COMPETITIVE ADVANTAGES OF BEING LEAN, SMALL, AND TRANSPARENT (WE'RE NOW FIGHTING A DIFFERENT KIND OF WAR)

I f you have been to Silicon Valley, have browsed through tech websites such as Mashable and TechCrunch, or even read your local newspaper, then you may have heard the term "startup" more often than you probably want.

Startups are the disruptors that we talked about in the previous chapter, the new, small companies that innovate and disrupt the larger, stagnant companies or industries. Just like the U. Military has had to become more lean, nimble, and strategic as threats have changed (from fighting large countries in WW2, for instance, to fighting the war on terror), so, too companies have to change in order to stay competitive—and fight this new kind of war.

So what is it about start-ups that make them more conducive to innovation? And what can we learn from their structure and culture how to better fight this new innovation war?

Characteristics of a New Kind of Army

I was once invited to a conference in the Valley, and while on a break, I decided to roam around and ended up wandering into a cafeteria. I was not the least surprise to see young adults, more than 85 percent of them seem to be barely out of university or college, huddled together with laptops and other mobile devices sitting in front of them. Many were serious, and some were heavily arguing. Regardless, the cafeteria was filled with euphoria and energy that usually comes with building something.

This vibrant scene—which reflects the start-up culture—reminded me of a TV show I like watching called *Silicon Valley*. It is basically a comedy about a startup that consists of five young guys trying to make it big in the holy grounds of tech, Silicon Valley, with their app called Pied Piper.

I am drawn to the show because of how it depicts startups. Although it is somewhat filled with stereotypes (not all tech people love to wear hoodies all the time. I happened to be in my suit at least three times in the past week for business meetings and conferences) many of those stereotypes hit close to home: the culture that is greatly inspired by tech giants such as Google, Apple, and Microsoft; the struggle to find enough money to build and launch a product; the lack of knowledge about how to run a tech company with a reliable business model; and the pain and rewards of creating a technology that is hopefully going to address the needs of consumers, whether they are already existent or not.

The show has definitely made me say, "Welcome to the world of startups!"

So what makes startups unique? "Startup" is defined in many different ways, depending on who you ask and in what context. Warby Parker's CEO and cofounder Neil Blumenthal defines a startup as an enterprise that is "working to solve a problem where the solution is not obvious and success is not guaranteed." Homejoy's CEO and cofounder Adora Cheung, on the other hand, thinks as startups as "a state of mind," where employees and its founders prefer to give more importance to quick and immediate impact of their products over stability or sustainability.

In a broad or general sense, startup is a fledgling business, an enterprise that is still in its early days or even years of operations. Thus, in truth, the term is not completely exclusive to tech companies. A coffee shop that has been in operation for five months is really not that different from an app company that has been set up for around a year.

Indeed, whether it is tech or any small business, it shares some of the most common characteristics:

They have been in business about three years or less

Startups are those businesses that have been created just recently. Once a company has been around for three to five years, which is usually the amount of time needed to determine if a business has become sustainable or not, it is often no longer considered new. By then, it should already be generating profits or maintain a positive cash outflow. It should also have experienced product growth and market expansion. Otherwise, if these goals have not been fulfilled, the company will cease to exist.

They have very limited funds

It's normal for any business just starting out to have limited funds. Entrepreneurs most prepared to do business are the ones who have accumulated months or years of personal savings, but we all know that it is never really enough even if you have made a really good business plan or feasibility study.

The same thing goes for tech startups—but most startups are built by younger individuals and teams who have had less time to accumulate savings. Most startups are built by individuals and teams who are 35 to 44 years old, followed by young adults between 26 and 34 years old, and around 4 percent of startups are developed by CEOs and founders (as well as co-founders) who are a mere 18 to 25 years old!

They have few employees

In the TV show, *Silicon Valley,* the startup Pied Piper is run by around five people, one of whom acts as a co-founder or partner since the product was developed in his home, which served as the incubation center. It is typical among startups to be almost a one-man (or one-woman) show. I have a friend who started his coffee shop in a run-down former fire department. Since he needed to renovate the place, about 60 percent of his savings was drained, leaving a very little room for marketing and, most of all, labor. So for the first few months, his crew was composed of his parents and his friends (including me) who were kind enough to spare at least two hours of our time to wait on tables and prepare some of the cups. It was an incredible experience that gave me a clear and honest idea of the challenges of operating a startup.

Tech Startups vs. Other Small Businesses

But then how different is a tech startup from all the other startups? At this point, let me recall what Paul Graham shared in an article "What Is a Startup?" by Natalie Robehmed. One of the distinct attributes of a tech startup and which differentiates it from other small businesses that are starting to operate is that the former has all the ability to achieve rapid expansion or growth because of the following reasons:

They are not bound by geography

An app, for example, can be downloaded by anyone anywhere as long as he has access to the Internet. Sometimes it is already a pre-set or downloaded app that adds more value to the mobile device. The product is also available twenty-four hours a day, seven days a week. There are a few things that can prevent that from happening, such as censorship of certain countries. Facebook and Twitter, for example, are prohibited in China. Ridiculous apps like Unexplainable X-rays and World's Biggest Porkchop have been 100 percent or nearly banned.

They tend to grow very fast

In fact, the speed in which it grows and becomes popular is one of the major considerations of investors, whether they are angel investors or venture capitalists. Along with the growth is the potential of generating very high revenues and very quick returns of investment. A case in point is Flappy Bird built by a sole app programmer. Before it was officially killed by its maker, it could already earn as much as $50,000 EVERY SINGLE DAY.

Why Are Employees Attracted to Startups?

Despite the limitation in the workforce, startups continue to attract people who wish to join these companies. I am a constant fixture in Startup Weekend—an event held in several cities around the world where tech entrepreneurs can pitch their startup ideas—for a number of reasons. First, I am constantly amazed on the amount of talent, creativity, and originality pitchers have. Of course, not all of the ideas are doable, and some of them are not worth considering at all, but nevertheless the thought process is really good. But many of the startup ideas possess the four "P's" of marketing, including the right **product**, at the right **price,** in the right **place**, with the right **promotion**, that set them up for success.

Second I love to see the energy and passion people have when it comes to startups. Over the years, we have seen the tremendous growth of participants that Startup Weekend is now being held in many countries.

What attracts talents to tech startups by the way?

A Cool Culture

In order for innovation to thrive, a company needs to have the right culture. Yahoo used to be one of the biggest tech brands in the world until it was plagued by poor leadership and management. It underwent a couple of changes in leadership until Marissa Mayer stepped in and introduced an actually old working concept but certainly alien to large companies: telecommuting.

Definitely Yahoo is no longer a startup considering the amount of time it has been around. Although it still struggles financially, it is already a big business. The idea of telecommuting, however, is common among startups as they try to reduce operating costs and simply maximize collaboration tools, some of which can already be accessed via a cloud.

Tech startups are often pictured as cool. All you need to do is to Google "Googleplex," the headquarters of one of the biggest companies in the world, to get an idea of what I mean: slides that connect second to first floors, free food, a large playground and a swimming pool, an open-door policy, etc. Again, this is no longer startup, but these have already become the metrics in which the startup culture is measured. The more relaxed it is, the more "startup" a business becomes.

A Lean Structure

Startups also have the capability of being lean. This is another ingredient to fostering innovation. Lean is a breakthrough concept in managing and building businesses and is basically one of the foundations of this book. Thus, I will discuss it extensively in the coming pages.

One of the advantages of a lean startup is it does not suffer from any kind of red tape or bureaucracy. As its name suggests, all methodologies are kept to bare essentials. The organization is almost flat, which helps speed up the decision-making process, and everyone is given a chance to contribute to the growth of the business. This is very powerful since it validates Abraham Maslow's hierarchy of needs: a person's greatest need is not actually money but self-actualization and recognition.

Tech startups are often criticized by the lack of benefits they provide to their employees. Although you can't expect stock options and pension plans right away, it is common among startups to offer "perks" in line with the culture I talked about earlier. For example, startups these days have a comprehensive pantry with free-flowing coffee and sometimes snacks like donuts or pizzas. Do not be surprised if they have "programs" like Friday beer nights or Wednesday movie dates.

Though it is tech, it also relies on creativity; and in order to encourage employees to be creative, analytical, and original, tech startups often advocate a very relaxed or laid-back dress code. In fact, some companies do not have any at all so it is quite normal for employees to come into the office in flip-flops and shorts—something they cannot easily do if they work in legacy or more traditional companies.

As startups, everybody plays a critical role; and as such, every person is compelled, pushed, and encouraged to contribute. Many tech startup CEOs promote a more open philosophy—that is, they allow their employees to provide an idea, take risks, and head projects from ideas they themselves conceive. This type of openness, which is usually missing in more complex organizations such as legacy companies, is more than enough to attract talents, from the creatives to the technicals.

Ingredients for Innovation

So put all of these characteristics together and they add up to companies that are young, agile, lean, cool, small, fast-growing, and mobile. Those are ingredients that spark innovation. Startups don't have a choice—they must innovate or fail. But that's also true of more established companies. Older companies must innovate, or risk becoming irrelevant or disrupted.

So what is an older company supposed to do, if they can't go back to being young, small, agile, and cool? What are the changes a more established company needs to make in order to spark innovation? In the next chapter, we'll talk more about how established companies can keep innovating and avoid stagnation.

Resources

- http://www.dr4ward.com/dr4ward/2012/01/who-works-for-a-startup-infographic.html
- http://startups.co.uk/5-advantages-of-working-for-a-start-up/

Chapter 7

APPLE & GOOGLE: HOW ESTABLISHED COMPANIES CAN KEEP INNOVATING (OR STAY IN THE FIGHT)

I n the 1990s, Stanford University Ph.D. students Larry Page and Sergey Brin thought they'd created the best thing since sliced bread. Their search engine intuitively worked on an algorithm that checked links to pages and served up results based on "popularity" and "authority" derived from that link data.

They offered it to Excite.com—asking only a million dollars for the idea and were turned down flat. The response was the same everywhere: not another search engine!

Then, in 1998, a meeting was arranged by Stanford professor David Cheriton with Andy Bechtolsheim, a co-founder of Sun Microsystems and well-known Silicon Valley investor. Bechtolsheim drove over to meet them— Page and Brin were desperate. If their idea failed to get funding, they were going to have to return to their Ph.Ds. They ran through a demonstration of how Google works, and showed the quality of the results versus search engine incumbents.

It was immediately clear to Bechtolsheim that Google had wings.

"I think this is the best idea I've seen in my entire life," said Bechtolsheim. He went to his car and when he came back he had his checkbook. He wrote a check for $100,000 to Page and Brin on the spot.

There was just one problem. Google didn't have a bank account yet.

"Put it in there when you do," Bechtolsheim said.

Now, twenty years later, Alphabet, Google's parent company, has grown into one of the most profitable companies in the US, according to *Fortune* magazine.

So how does a company like Google, and Apple, which is also one of the world's most successful brands, remain innovative decades later? How do large, established companies continue to innovate and compete with the more agile, lean startups?

To answer that question, let's start by acknowledging the differences between start-ups and established companies, and then let's look at Google and Apple, and the ways they continue to innovate.

The Differences Between Startups and Established Companies

Growing vs Improving

Startups have one job, which is to grow. Growing means getting bigger, adding competency, and intensifying operations and reach. But established companies have a different job. They improve on what they have built. Their objective is to squeeze the greatest out of the existing business models, to master effectiveness, and convey more value to shareholders by exploiting more with what they already have.

Startups are forced to grow through hacks and innovations. Established companies may continue to grow, but it's through either buying smaller companies, or by internal innovations within the existing model.

Fixed Business Model vs Experimentation

The type of business model is another difference between start-ups and legacy companies. Large enterprises are classically focused on implementing sales using a known business model, wherein startups are in the grand quest for a business model that works.

One of the most significant things early-stage ventures do is to experiment with different business models until they find the one that works for them. Larger enterprises are more fixed in their business model and, having found a product market suitable and sustainable, are likely to make less intense changes. They don't want to fix what isn't broken.

Consequently, as the dynamic is changing, larger enterprises are being forced by emerging technologies and fast-changing markets to make business model innovation a matter of urgency.

Risk Seeking vs Risk Averse

Startups are built to take risks. The odds are against startups from the early stages of their ventures, so risk-taking is deep-rooted. Taking risks is the only way a startup venture can be fast enough to cross the gap and break through.

Rather than actively seeking out risk, established companies look at risk contrarily, and are in fact designed to lower and manage risk and make decisions to improve return.

This pattern and tendency is seen throughout nature: just as a child is more likely to take risks to explore the world around them, an adult is much more likely to be aware of potential folly.

A Case Study: Google and Apple

Despite their disadvantages when it comes to innovation, established companies *can* still innovate. Let's look at how two established companies, Apple and Google, have defied the odds by not allowing themselves to stagnate.

Between them, Apple and Google have dominated and shaped the platform technology industry for the past decade. In many ways the companies seem identical—the digital Mary-Kate and Ashley Olsen of our day—and many of their product offerings even sound, well, the same: Apple Pay. Android Pay. Apple Photos. Google Photos. Apple Wallet. Google Wallet. You get the drift.

Yet pull back the shroud and you'll see they've shaped their identities on genuinely individual innovation models.

Instances of Innovation

Google, as a startup, originally advanced on the basis of a simple, fast search engine which affords high-quality responses. Now, as an established company, the product pallet has become more diverse over time with Gmail, Google News, Google Images, the Froogle price comparison service, the Google Chrome internet browser, the Android operating system, Google Maps and Google Earth map tools and Google TV (superseded by Android TV).

Once it matured as a company, Google continued to grow and remain innovative through an intense buyout program to obtain smaller companies for their emerging technologies and know-how such as YouTube ($1.65 billion), AdMob ($681 million), Double Click ($3.2 billion), Grand Central (future Google Voice), and Keyhole (future Google earth). These other companies haven't always appeared on face value to be linked in any obvious way to the core business of Google's search expertise, but are all driven by technological challenge, and the opportunity of taking innovation further to provide a different, useful, and effective service online.

On the other hand, Apple has remained competitive through internal innovation and focusing on their core product offering. Apple has built its achievement on its renowned Macintosh whose GUI revolutionized computing. Apple transformed the business model originated by IBM in many ways— by purchasing its parts such as microprocessors from external dealers, using a network of stores as outlets for its computers and targeting both the public at large and professional users. Apple has managed consistency even when enlarging its product-line from PC to other entertainment devices, and has always maintained a strong innovation focus. Despite copyright battles with the Beatles Apple Corps over their use of the Apple brand in the music industry, Apple Inc's iTunes music and video download service debuted in 2003 helping the company develop into a true content provider.

The Process of Innovation

Google believes that people are more creative when they work on things they consider important or they have created. This is a great way of stimulating bottom-up innovation. Consequently, people discuss what they are working on over coffee or lunch at the Google Café, while the Google intranet encourages employees to share what they're working on right now. Employees can directly email any of the company's leaders.

Google also sets aside time for meetings where engineers can listen to any feedback their colleagues have about their potential ideas. A positive response means that other people are ready to work with you and can be the first phase in constituting a new project. Some of these ideas indeed go on to receive funding and management support. At Google good ideas—ideas that include the right product, in the right place, at the right time, with the right promotion—are encouraged no matter an employee's rank. "We try to have as many channels for expression as we can, recognizing that different people, and different ideas, will percolate up in different ways," says Laszlo Bock, Senior Vice President of Google's People Operations.

In contrast, Apple creates self-contained environments around its products. The software is an integral part of the hardware and any disconnection between the software and the appearance of the terminal could damage the brand. Apple has mastered the art of the brand as a story; they have created such a compelling story around their brand that many consumers want to be a part of it.

Apple also doesn't hesitate to execute takeovers in order to save time, acquire expertise or complete the network surrounding their innovations. With the purchase of PA Semi, a chip designer, along with the grey matter of its employees, Apple has maintained a competitive advantage for its tablet and iPhone in terms of energy efficiency, performance and production costs. But Apple buyouts are still fewer than Google. Apple still likes innovation to be in-house.

Linked to that Apple innovation process is the privacy which surrounds the design and launch of new products. Apple executives are well schooled in its strategy of silence; certain rooms are shielded from the eyes of inquisitive employees and projects are labelled by code names. It all creates a mystery that something big is happening. And it better be—that is just what consumers who have brought into the Apple story are expecting.

Many of these innovative practices have been copied by other organizations, but far too often the copycat misses the point of an exercise. It's why we see so many corporate innovation labs today with bean bags, coffee machines, and yoga. The aesthetics are only the visible 'tangible' ways in which Apple and Google are different. But the core of their success goes much deeper than bean bags and yoga.

Designed for Users

Google's search engine is characterized by an extremely simple homepage in terms of design. This page was originally designed by Sergey Brin (who has no great artistic talent), as a result of lack of money needed to pay a graphic artist. Google's initial method to design was to a certain degree unplanned in which pleasing results arrive by chance. The same simplicity is found in products that followed: Google Earth, Gmail, Chrome, etc. in which the main purpose of the graphical user interface is to meet a need of the user and the design is therefore unobtrusive.

Apple shares this design ascetic. Its products have constantly been cleanly designed and easy to use. Apple is great at figuring out how to reinvent existing technology and make it much more user friendly. While creators of other MP3 players were stacking their products with new features, Apple launched the iPod, that's key features were stripped down simplicity and ease of use. "Design." Steve Jobs said, "is not just what it looks like and feels like. Design is how it works."

Business Model

While Google could be seen as a company operating an advertising-based service model, what it actually did was take the yellow pages of the phone directory and put it online. It was this innovative move which cemented Google as the preeminent search engine. Rather than pay the yellow pages for a listing by industry and name, it's now keywords that drive internet search and so businesses pay for keyword-rich ads. The model of selling keyword advertising was pioneered by the directory based Goto.com (later renamed Overture Services, before being acquired by Yahoo!) but Google was certainly among the first companies to see a clear monetary value in keyword search, and find ways to turn the business model on its head. While many search engine predecessors stalled (Altavista, anyone? How about Hotbot?) Google quietly rose in stature while continuing to generate astonishing revenue.

The Apple business model remains fairly typical for a manufacturer marketing its own terminals and accessories. This has recently been complemented by the online iTunes facility (video rent payment and music sales), the applications available in the App Store (revenue distributed with the application designers) and the Apple Store distribution network (recovery of distributor margins), with Apple spreading its control over the industry network.

Masters of Innovation

To flourish, a company must be a master of innovation. Innovative leaders do not only start innovative companies; they sustain them with continuous growth. No two companies get this better than Apple and Google, which have become titans of their industries.

Can they continue? Well, maybe. It's certainly the case that large corporations serve two masters—the risk-averse stock market and the risk-desiring consumer. Even with many concessions by the companies, many brilliant minds at both have flown the coop to work for startups for exactly this reason. It becomes much harder to let creativity bloom fully within a risk-averse environment.

Some would argue that we are seeing the transformation of Apple today under the leadership of Tim Cook from a startup mindset to a much more cautious corporate entity, relying much on upgrades to existing products rather than innovative product launches. Steve Jobs had a reputation for being capable of almost anything—occasional mistakes (LISA anyone?) or passionate, inspired decisions. Jobs remains the poster-boy for the young start-up founder.

But despite what the future holds for these two companies, there's no doubt they have set the benchmark for any established company to strive for if they want to continue to innovative, thrive, and survive.

Chapter 8

SOCIAL MEDIA, OPEN SOURCE TECHNOLOGY, AND OTHER TOOLS OF THE REVOLUTION

E ach great war is fought with a new set of technologies. And so it goes with an innovation war. Henry Ford fought his innovation war with the assembly line. Steve Jobs and Apple fought theirs with user-centered design principles. From firmly established technologies (social media and the public cloud) to trends that are demonstrating with each passing day that they are here to say (blockchain and artificial intelligence), let's discuss the technologies that are providing a toolkit for innovation, the building blocks that allow companies to deploy resources at a pace and scale never seen before.

Social Media

Social media is a force every business today must reckon with. The core value behind social media is something called **democratized opinion**. What does this mean? That no matter how esoteric or niche your interests or passions, social media now provides you with a means to easily connect with other like-minded people. If your hobby is weaving coconut leaf baskets underwater in scuba gear, there's a Facebook group for that—and it's several thousand members deep.

Social media allows us to engage in a dialog on everything and anything, at scale, with no overriding institution to control or govern it.

Social media and online forums have also transformed advertising into more of a two-way street. Go back twenty years and revisit the ad for a bank—it would have told you how safe your money is with them, and how they would provide the best return on your investment. But this messaging would have taken place in one direction: the brand talking to you, with effectively no opportunity for feedback or dialogue on that messaging.

But now, in the age of social media and omnipresent online engagement, consumers are empowered to engage with and evaluate the validity of a brand's messaging. One key example is the early "review" sites—like Trip Advisor and Four Square—which did something novel: they allowed consumers to provide feedback on brands and their products and services. This approach was quickly adopted by even larger players like Facebook and Google (such as with Google Maps) and many others.

But perhaps the best example of this at scale is the Amazon rankings and reviews engine. On Amazon, you can't just *say* you have the best product; the market has to agree. And this can make or break your product, based on whether the market actually agrees if it's any good or not.

Did you know that many cafes and restaurants around the world now make their food more photogenic? Why? Because Instagram marketing is so important. Social media has become a vital force in terms of creating a two-way dialog with the market and helping organizations understand if they are being truly responsive and responsible to their audiences and markets, by crafting messages that resonate and building products that add value to people's lives. This takes us back to the principle of **objective customer empathy**. Brands need to ensure that they are continually tapping into customer needs and desires and addressing those needs in their products and services.

The massive data-gathering potential of social media also provides a low-cost testing ground for new product features and services. It's no secret that companies like Google and Apple use social media to deliberately leak information about intended features and functions of upcoming devices and software, then use market response to justify the development of those features. If a leaked feature is received negatively, they'll use that feedback to de-prioritize or revisit that element of their product or service. If the response is overwhelmingly positive, that's a good signal to make that feature a development priority.

Of course, the data-gathering and consumer engagement potential of social media can be dangerous if it's not wielded carefully. It's easy for companies to get distracted by the "shiny object" of social media and the scope and immediacy of the market data available to them through these channels.

For any company in this day and age, social media strategy and engagement needs to be approached as seriously as any other part of the business. Thanks to social media, just about any brand messaging or activity that takes place online has now become a two-way dialog. This is the reality that brands must embrace and learn from. This new paradigm creates a huge opportunity and leverage for brands to succeed—or fail.

The Democratization of Programming

In the 18th century, Ada Lovelace wrote the world's very first computer program—a set of instructions designed to carry out a specific function or functions—for calculating Bernoulli's Number using the Analytical Engine.

Since then, hundreds, if not thousands, of programming languages have been created—much like the languages we use to communicate in written and spoken form each day, with their own rules and syntax—that can be used to create new programs. The earliest of these languages required coding in the form of binary digits—0s and 1s, messages sent directly to the computer's hardware. Known as low-level languages, they offered no layer of abstraction that would allow a human to conceive of their code in normal human-language terms; coders literally had to think like a machine.

But an evolution has occurred toward simplicity of programming languages, which has made programming or coding more accessible. We've come far since the early days, with practically every programming language in use today considered a *high-level* language that doesn't require coders to "think like a machine" but instead to craft programs using instructions that possess a more recognizable syntax.

Nowadays, many of the most popular languages are also some of the easiest to learn and implement. Two key examples are PHP and Python, which are extremely widely used, as well as some of the most user-friendly languages to learn and implement. That is not to say that every popular programming language in use today is user-friendly. But many of them are. And just as importantly, the scope of programming languages available today also means that there is a programming language for every use case. Some languages are better for web development, like Javascript and Ruby; languages like Python and R are ideal for statistical analysis. Java and C++ are well suited to developing full-featured applications.

Open Source Technologies

"Open source" is a term used to refer to technologies that are modifiable by anyone because their design is publicly accessible and modifiable. As such, open source technologies are a bedrock of enabling the agility that allows innovation to thrive. They reduce the barriers or latency, that can prevent a company from bringing its purpose to market in a timely manner.

Software is a technology that lends itself especially to being open source, because it is so easily modifiable. Open-source software (OSS) is computer software with its source code made available with a license in which the copyright holder provides the rights to study, change, and distribute the software to anyone and for any purpose. Open-source software may be developed in a collaborative public manner.

The open source model grew in popularity after Eric Raymond published the book *The Cathedral and the Bazaar* in 1997. In the startup community, developers have gravitated hugely toward open source tools—databases, coding technologies, and engineering libraries—to build their products and services, because these technologies are cheaper and faster to employ than closed source technologies.

Many programming languages themselves are even open source. PHP and Python, mentioned above, are two of the biggest ones, and Java, another of the most popular programming languages in the world, is partly open source.

Here are some of the key benefits open source software offers individuals and businesses. It's usually cheaper than traditional "locked-down" software. Security flaws in open source applications tend to be patched quickly because they are visible to all. Users have a hand in software development, Users and businesses also have the freedom and flexibility to customize the software to suit their needs, which can make the software more useful and of higher quality.

Blockchain

Perhaps the most notable open source technology, one with the promise to change something as elemental as *the recording of value*, is blockchain technology.

What blockchain does is allow for the deinstitutionalization of ledgers—a permanent account book in which transactions and records of value can be entered and stored. Blockchain creates an immutable ledger that does not rely on a third party or middleman—like a bank—to record and verify transactions and establish a historical record of value for something.

Blockchain has most famously been used as a mechanism for currency transactions. Witness the emergence of cryptocurrencies like Bitcoin and several others. As of the writing of this book, Bitcoin was undergoing a massive surge in valuation. The price of one bitcoin, after hovering in the range of $300–700 for three years, skyrocketed to more than $15,000. This possibly represents a speculative bubble, but the interest in Bitcoin is driving adoption and acceptance of the underlying blockchain technology.

Whether the future of currency transactions will be with Bitcoin and similar innovations is yet to be seen—but the blockchain's immense potential as an engine of innovation is not limited to a medium of monetary transactions. As Don Tapscott, CEO of the Tapscott Group, wrote in a blog post in July 2017, "Innovators are programming this new digital ledger to record anything of value to humankind—birth and death certificates, marriage licenses, deeds and titles of ownership, rights to intellectual property, educational degrees, financial accounts, medical history, insurance claims, citizenship and voting privileges, location of portable assets, provenance of food and diamonds, job recommendations and performance ratings, charitable donations tied to specific outcomes, employment contracts, managerial decision rights and anything else that we can express in code."

Although we're still in early days, blockchain technology is not going anywhere, and it has the potential to revolutionize the financial services industry the way the Internet revolutionized the media industry.

Public Cloud

Public cloud technology is another development that has significantly lowered the barriers to entry for a business to fight an innovation war on its own terms.

A public cloud is one in which a service provider makes resources, such as server storage, virtual machines (VMs), and even applications, available over the internet for public use, either for free or on a paid model. Public cloud resources reduce or eliminate the need for organizations to invest in and maintain their own computing and information technology resources on-site. Public cloud systems also allow for efficiency and scalability; an organization only uses what they need, and can easily increase their use of these resources as their needs change.

While not considered completely open source, public cloud technology has been a game-changer in allowing both small and large organizations to focus their energy and resources on innovation—instead of acquiring and maintaining an elaborate IT infrastructure. The cloud model of computing has revolutionized the sharing of electronic resources, be it storage, processing power, or applications.

And thanks to economies of scale, the cost of entry for public cloud technology are very low. If you have only a credit card available, you can spin up a bunch of Amazon Web Service servers at the size of Bank of America and deploy large-scale applications very quickly.

Artificial Intelligence and Big Data

An *Economist* cover story from May 2017 put it in stark terms: "The world's most valuable resource is no longer oil, but data." We have access to more data than ever before, and the increasing ability to derive meaning and value from that data: to store it, analyze it, manipulate it, and drive business intelligence from it.

There are three key factors at work here:

- There's more data available—hence the term "big data. " Technology is making it cheaper and easier to collect more data. Even previously analog data—paper-based data, is coming online at a furious pace.

- Increases in computing power and the low cost of data storage have made it possible to affordably manage and analyze these huge quantities of data. Instead of relying on data samples, organizations can now look at the data en masse to drive business decision-making.

- The growth of artificial intelligence (AI) and machine learning provides a mechanism to process and extract meaning from this data at scale, without human intervention.

The upshot? Businesses have a huge ability to gather data about their customers, and to analyze that data in ways not previously possible. The businesses that can wield this to the greatest advantage are well positioned to win their innovation war.

In the age of Facebook and Google, there's been much talk about the notion that the product–consumer paradigm has been flipped on its head. Sites like these two have come to dominate the world because they have established ecosystems that provide them with unprecedented access to the personal data of their users in exchange for largely free access to their services. As a *Wired* article title put it way back in 2011, "You are Facebook's product, not customer." It's the unspoken quid pro quo of the information age.

In 2012, John Rockefeller, chairman of the Senate Commerce Committee into data brokers, pointed out how easily the "unprecedented amount" of personal, medical and financial information available could be collected, mined and sold, to the potential detriment of consumers. He expressed a widely shared concern that "an ever-increasing percentage of their lives will be available for download, and the digital footprint they will inevitably leave behind will become more specific and potentially damaging, if used improperly."

But is this a generational thing? Statistics suggest that Gen Y are increasingly open with their data if their data being used for their own gain in what is known as a "value exchange." It's this comfort—the quid pro quo mentioned above—

that powers the buzz around platforms like Facebook, Twitter, LinkedIn, and the large majority of the viral networks that have become a part of daily life.

This "unprecedented amount" of personal, medical and financial data does create a digital footprint, and there are some risks that need to be managed. But, we also have to realize that this "footprint" opens the door for the ability to do something never before possible. Thanks to big data and artificial intelligence, organizations are faced with the opportunity to create a "data-driven serendipity," where they know their customer well enough to design experiences that delight, using highly intelligent algorithms that leverage the insight of that customer's digital "footprint."

Destination: Innovation

There is a final layer that makes all of these tools even more powerful, accelerating their adoption and therefore their impact. It is the growing ability for people everywhere to essentially learn almost anything from anywhere at anytime. This phenomenon is leading to more rapid adoption of technologies and acquisition of skills across the board. In the past, for instance, to learn computer science you had to go to a university and do a three-year degree program. Today, however, you can jump online and learn from a series of YouTube videos or a Udemy course. It's targeted learning, it's accessible, and it allows a person to learn an entirely new skill very quickly. From coding, to the cloud, to blockchain, the playing field has been leveled.

Like any tools, these technologies can be wielded by organizations as a force for true innovation, or innovation theater—the appearance of innovation without the rigorous authenticity of actual innovation. Not every forward-looking company will need to engage equally with each of these technologies as they build their strategy and amass resources for winning their innovation war—some may turn more to social media while others put their eggs in the basket of big data and AI. But chances are that all of these technologies, to some degree, will be part of the toolkit that helps organizations large and small establish a strategic advantage in the years to come. Consider yourself warned.

Chapter 9

FUNDING THE ARMS RACE: VENTURE CAPITAL TO CROWDFUNDING

A s someone who's spent considerable time in the banking sector, I keep a close watch on trends in this wider space. And I'm particularly interested in forms of funding that have emerged in recent years. In order to innovate, you need talent, yes, but you also need the fuel of money to drive the process. I see two major trends fueling innovation from a financing perspective: the rise of corporate venture capital, and of crowdfunding.

Corporate Venture Capital

Corporate venture capital (CVC) is defined as the act of venturing into a corporate agreement by investing funds directly into a starting company (startup), known in a CVC context as the "portfolio company." Investments like these often suggest that these larger companies are not only motivated by investing funds but by strategically investing in goals that will further their business. These larger firms invest in smaller companies in the hopes of benefiting in the form of increased profits, strategic advantage, and the acquisition of new ideas and technologies.

This venture also lets big companies function on a smaller scale, allowing them to innovate faster and discover which opportunities are viable. Corporations use their vast influence in the business grounds to locate new markets and opportunities that can in turn develop their current businesses.

The goal of CVC may be to enhance the parent company's financial objectives, strategic objectives, or both.

In financially-driven CVC investments, the parent or main firm targets leverage on returns, usually via sales of stakes to a third party or parties, initial public offerings (IPOs), or other exits. The firm aims to make use of the profit and independent revenue in the new business venture itself. The portfolio company could also be creating a capability that improves profitability for the parent company, particularly when build a new asset that might optimise or enhance an existing P&L.

CVC investments that are strategically driven aim to directly or indirectly increase the profits and sales of the firm's *current* business. The firm seeks to capitalize on a sort of symbiotic relationship between itself and the new business venture in order to improve its own strategic standing. It can be useful to view these kinds of investments as not just strategically driven, but strategy *creating*, enabling the exploration of *new* strategic options for the firm. And of course, when a strategically motivated investment decision pays off, it may result in financial gain for the parent company, as well.

Despite the similar names, CVC is not synonymous with venture capital (VC). Rather, CVC is a subset or special form of VC. A venture capital firm raises investment money through institutional investors or individual investors, while CVC involves using the cash reserves of the parent firm to fund the startup business. There is more pressure to generate profit and returns from traditional venture capital. In CVC, the venture is often regarded as research and development (R&D), with less resulting pressure to generate a profit. In addition, most often, a CVC division has a competitive advantage over a private VC firm because of its extensive knowledge on new technologies and marketing strategies.

Disadvantages

Although corporate venture capital has become an important driver of innovation in multiple industries it can also pose some risks.

One of the disadvantages is the potential for conflicts of business interest between the larger firm and the startup company. Take, for example, an insurance company, where its core business is to categorize and exclude risk. But in a world of abundant data and computing power, it's very possible that a startup could develop a way to implement preventative analytics that mitigate risks, challenging the core commercial model of insurance. While the incumbent company may to want to explore alternative business models like this, their investor relationship may limit the experimentation.

In contrast, relatively young companies that are still under the process of development may have issues with the huge impact a bigger corporations may bring to their business. Also, if the startup company were to suddenly shift direction in a way that conflicted with the aims of their corporate investor, the investor may withdraw its support or may end their agreement.

Types and Stages of CVC Investing and Financing

Let's explore in more detail the types of investments that fall under the umbrella of CVC, including the process and stages of financing stages in a CVC arrangement.

Professor Henry Chesbrough of Haas School of Business states that CVC has two trademarks or hallmarks, namely:

- Its objective
- The extent of connection between the investing and operations of start-up company.

There are generally acknowledged to be four broad types of CVC investment strategy that capture the range of objectives and extent of connection between the two companies in any given CVC arrangement: driving investments, enabling investments, emergent investments, and passive investments.

Driving Investments

When the investment firm's business operation is very similar or tightly linked to the startup company, this is called a driving investment. The investment firm will often look at the potential growth of the startup company and then combine it with the parent company with the purpose of strategically advancing both the parent firm and the startup company. However, this type of CVC investment has its limits. The link between the investment company and the startup may make it difficult to recognize new opportunities for growth. Not relying too much on driving investments may be a good idea if the company wants to break out of its mold and explore newer strategies and processes.

Enabling Investments

This type of investment is the opposite of a driving investment. The venture is not tightly linked with the parent firm's business. Companies that engage in enabling investments see less need for a strong operational link between the parent company and the startup business to achieve success. It is also a strategic move by the investment company because it can take advantage of complementary products and services it may already offer to create demand for the products and services of the startup firm.

Emergent Investments

Emergent investments are similar to driving investments since the venture is tightly linked to the investing company's business operation. The venture for the startup business serves as an "option" strategy for the investing company, in which a change in the business environment could make the investment venture strategically valuable. Most often, emergent investments are directed at unrelated, untapped markets that the company is not yet able to enter because they are still focused on their current market. Initially, the investment is just for financial gain, but if a venture proves to be successful, the investing company may shift their core focus toward this new direction.

Passive Investments

The sole purpose of a passive investment is profit and financial gain. This venture is not linked to the business operation of the investing company and it serves no strategic purpose for the company. Most companies avoid this type of CVC investment because it does not provide any strategic advantage.

CVC Financing: The Stages

Startup companies go through various phases of development, and CVC firms can provide the funding for each phase of development. Each development phase has its individual financing requirements; when working with a startup, a CVC will help determine the requisite financing stage as well as their preferred type of investments to make.

Early Stage Financing: The startup company essentially has an idea or concept in this stage. Capital is exhausted for product development and market research. The company can use startup financing to set up research and development, management, quality management, and marketing teams. It can also use this financing to purchase additional resources and equipment.

First-Stage Financing: The extension of early-stage financing is called first-stage financing. This is where companies begin to manufacture their products and devise sales processes to initiate product launches.

Seed Capital Funds: The startup is still forming its idea or concept in this phase, and service and production still need more time to ripen. The investment money during this period can be used to create an operational prototype. The funds can also be utilized to carry out additional market research.

Second-Stage Expansion Financing: In this stage, companies that are already marketing and selling their products are funded to help them expand their business. The provided funds, typically between one and ten million dollars, can be used to recruit additional workers to set up sales, engineering, and marketing functions. Companies that are not making profits can also use the funds to offset their negative cash flow.

Third-Stage Mezzanine Financing: Mezzanine financing is most beneficial when it comes to business expansion. The funds can be used for advancement of marketing and management, construction of factories, and production of additional products. Most companies at this stage are operating stably, even managing to break even or gain some profits.

Initial Public Offering (IPO)

An initial public offering or IPO is when the startup company's stock is offered to the public. It is what CVCs often describe as the ideal scenario, as this is when an investing company can, at long last, start to earn a substantial ROI. An IPO is often the last point of a CVC's involvement. They sell their stock, then they look for fresh ventures to reinvest their money. The whole cycle repeats itself with a new startup company.

Mergers and Acquisitions

There are times when the economic climate creates a scarcity of IPO opportunities, and venture capital firms have no choice but to look to mergers and acquisitions. This is the best option to make when a venture capital firm can see that a startup company has no feasible plan of functioning independently. Acquisition financing makes use of the funds or investment to buy or acquire a different company. The venture capital firms complete it by aligning their startup with a business line or complementary product that can lead to smooth integration of the combined companies. The objective is to create more advantages and benefits.

Acquisition works both ways—another firm could still acquire the invested startup. In this scenario, the CVC would gain cash when it sells its investment and use the capital gains to reinvest in a new business venture.

Mergers bear similarities to acquisitions, with the only difference being that neither company buys the other one. The two companies, in this case, are combining and sharing their resources, technology, and processes for their common benefit. Both companies look forward to better market positioning, cost savings, and liquidity. Fundraising efforts and other problems are also shared, which effectively cuts the burden of each company in half.

The stages presented above are only the basic ones; each CVC has its own financing stages. Startup companies need to understand and weigh whether the financing strategies offered by the CVC they work with can help them achieve their goals.

CVC Financing: The Process

Below are the basic steps that are usually done by investing companies, from the initial contact with the startup business company until the first round of financing.

First Stage: First Contact

The process starts when the startup company comes into contact with the investing company or CVC. Sometimes, it's the other way around: large companies seek out startup companies that need funding.

Second Stage: Presentation of Business Plan and Product Demonstration

A meeting is held between the investing company and the startup company. The startup's management team will thoroughly present their business plan to the CVC. If the CVC is still interested, the startup will proceed with a product demonstration. In order to fully understand the startup company's business and product offering, the investing company will then do its own research and investigation.

Third Stage: Determining the Value of the Startup

If the investing company is interested in the product or service of the startup company, they will proceed to determine the value of the startup. The valuation is presented to the startup company using a term sheet, and the offer is then studied and evaluated by the startup company. If the offer is acceptable, both parties can then agree on an investor equity and purchase price. Both sides can negotiate during this stage.

Fourth Stage: Lock Up Time Period

Both parties, represented by their legal counsel, finalize the term sheet. This is also a lock-up time period where the startup company cannot go to other investment groups to discuss investment opportunities. When the term sheet is finalized, both parties can then talk about the financing terms.

Fifth Stage: Thorough Investigation of the Startup Company

This stage involves the thorough investigation of the startup company. Negotiations are still continuing between the legal counsels of both sides, addressing all outstanding issues. The CVC can investigate the financial records, employees, suppliers, and customer base of the startup company.

Sixth Stage: Closing of Financing

The closing of financing is the final stage of the financing process. It takes place after the execution of the agreement.

World Leaders Putting CVC to Work

CVC isn't just a theoretical framework—it's a model being used by some of the largest and most successful companies in the world to expand and enhance their strategic footholds and develop new and innovative technologies, products, and services.

A number of large firms have used CVC to invest in startups to seek breakthroughs in medicine, telecommunications, science, and information and communication technologies. We'll look at a few of those companies.

Healthcare: GlaxoSmithKline and Takeda Pharmaceutical Company

Perhaps the two most notable examples in the healthcare industry for CVC investments are GlaxoSmithKline (GSK) and Takeda Pharmaceutical Company (TPC). Both companies have used CVC to invest in startups in the fields of medical care, life science, biotechnology, medicine, and many others. In the fields of medicine and health, continuing innovation and breakthroughs are very important, for the obvious reason of developing new drugs and medical devices that will help patients, and also to help these companies be profitable. This is a major reason companies like GSK and TPC are continuously looking for smaller companies that present opportunities that can vastly improve medical science.

The venture arms of these two companies see themselves as financial investors in different areas of interest. They usually target small companies that are closely related to the parent company but have a much broader focus. Although these companies, like almost every company in the broader healthcare industry (especially pharmaceuticals), have their own R&D department, they may find benefit through seeking investment opportunities with startups that are pushing the envelope even further.

GSK has two main CVC components: a venture fund, SR One, and a strategic venture capital fund called the Action Potential Venture Capital (APVC). SR One invests in emerging life science companies that focus on science innovations and improvements in medical care. This firm has already invested over $800 million in biotechnology groups. APVC, launched in 2013, invests specifically in companies working on bioelectronic medicines all over the world.

TPC's venture capital arm is called Takeda Research Investment (TRI). TRI has invested in three companies with the potential for significant scientific and technological discoveries. The first is Lectus Therapeutics, a UK-based biotech company that has discovered a process to develop unique molecules that modulate ion channels. The second is a California-based pharmaceutical company called Adams Pharmaceuticals that focuses on the treatment of neurological disorders. The third company is Xenon, a Canadian bio-pharmaceutical company working on different treatments for human diseases that isolate the genes that underlie these disorders, so that they can create drugs to target these genes.

Information and Communication Technologies : Chevron and Samsung

ICT stands for Information and Communication Technologies. It is a collective term for any technological equipment, resources, and applications, used mainly to communicate, and to generate, distribute, retrieve, save and manipulate information. These include the Internet, computers, radio, television, satellite systems, etc.

Chevron is one of the leading multinational energy companies in the world. Although primarily an energy company, technological advancement plays a key role in Chevron's overall business as the company aims to develop technologies that can drive global socio-economic advancement. Supporting Chevron's global operations are three technology-based companies, Chevron Technology Company, Chevron Technology Ventures, and Chevron Information Technology Company. Chevron Technology Ventures aims to incorporate new technologies into its operational processes. This is made possible by Chevron Venture Capital, which researches companies all over the world to find the ones that might provide a significant economic return.

Started as a small trading company, Samsung has evolved into one of the world's leading ICT companies. Samsung's venture wing, Samsung Venture Investment Corporation, specializes in funding smaller companies that typically focus on information and communication, software, internet, electronics, displays, in life science and healthcare, movie and video sectors, semiconductor, connected device, remote computing, cyber security, mobile devices and many more. It generally expands its influence overseas, from Asia to North America to Europe.

Utilities and Telecom Companies: Deutsche Telekom and KT Corporation

Deutsche Telekom, or German Telecom, was a state-owned corporation until its privatization in the mid-'90s. It holds significant shares in other telecom companies such as Slovak Telecom (Slovakia), Magyar Telekom (Hungary), and T-Hrvatski (Croatia) among others.

T-Venture is Deutsch Telekom's venture capital company. Founded in 1997, T-Venture is considered to be one of the leading corporate venture capital companies in the world, having invested in almost 200 companies worldwide to date. One of the company's visions is to help startups and young, fast-growing companies in become established and successful.

KT Corporation, formerly Korean Telecom, is South Korea's largest telecommunications service provider. The company, which claims almost 100 percent of the country's landline and broadband internet subscribers, pioneered the nation's transformation into a center of information technology innovation. Its venture capital arm, SK Telecom Ventures, targets investments in early- to mid-stage companies in the areas of telecommunications, semiconductor, consumer Internet, IT infrastructure, mobility, and enterprise solutions, from all across the globe.

Media: Naspers

One of the most well-known and influential companies in the media sector that utilizes corporate venture capital is Naspers, an South Africa-based business founded in 1915 that is currently the largest local company on the Johannesburg Stock Exchange. Once an influential mouthpiece for apartheid, Naspers has grown and owns a multitude of media assets in South Africa, which includes more than 50 domestic newspapers and pay TV. It is one of the earliest investor in Facebook and the majority shareholder of Tencent Holdings, China's leading internet group. Naspers utilizes a blend of venture capital, as well as an operating company that funds, acquires, builds and scales tech businesses in the areas of advertising, social media, online gaming, mobile commerce, and more, in various regions of the globe.

Financial: Citigroup

Companies that offer financial services, such as banks and insurers, have long been active limited partners in providing capital funds to independent business ventures. Banks have been tagged as important private equity investors for a long time. However, their motivations for investment pursuit are usually more complex than the investment activity of other limited partners.

Banks sometimes invest in venture capital to acquire initial access to companies they are interested in before the companies conduct an IPO. According to the results of the research of Global Corporate Venturing, there are fewer financial services, including banks, which remain active in the financial sector. The possible reasons are the number of IPOs has seen significant decrease since the dot-com boom, poor financial returns over the past years, and regulatory restrictions.

However, the insurer called The Hartford and the bank known as Citigroup started to engage in corporate venturing. The Hartford has invested in three companies to date. In November 2010, Citigroup was awarded the title of "most influential corporate venturing unit in financial services" from Global Corporate Venturing.

In addition, Citigroup has invested millions in the Communities at Work Fund to assist small businesses to acquire loans, develop new community centers, and renovate housing units.

Energy/Clean Tech: Dow Venture Capital

Clean technology focuses on power consumption reduction or efficiency improvement by using wireless or digital products to produce cost-efficient energy. Clean technology is known as the "first global technological revolution" according to the Cleantech Group, a company that supports the development and marketability of clean technologies.

The Cleantech Group has also seen significant increase in corporate venturing in energy and clean technology in the past few years.

Dow Venture Capital (DVC) is the CVC arm of Dow Chemical Company, one of the biggest chemical companies in the world, with $60 billion in sales. DVC invests in or partners with many companies in various sectors of cleantech. DVC is focused on strategic investments that help accelerate the business growth of Dow, and also add value to the portfolio companies.

DVC invests in businesses and technologies that offer promise at addressing some of the world's most challenging issues, including renewable energy production and preservation, clean water sourcing, and increased agricultural production.

Conclusion

The importance of corporate venture capital in the world of business cannot be discounted. It is a very efficient way for start-up companies to get financing and aid in their development.

It is important to remember that corporate venture capital has a combination of financial and strategic objectives. These give rise to numerous investment strategies and different stages of financing; the end goal of which is a return on investment. There are various advantages that corporate venture capital brings to many sectors, especially in the telecommunication and software sectors. These advantages serve as determining factors that make corporate venture capital more preferable as compared to venture capital financing.

Crowdfunding

There's another form of financing that's fueling the innovation wars: crowdfunding. Crowdfunding is the use of the Internet by small businesses or individuals to raise capital to support the development of products or services through limited investments from a large number of investors.

Crowdfunding has emerged alongside similar models like microfinance (loans to help people in poverty), and peer-to-peer lending (for-profit financial transactions between individuals) as a way of bypassing traditional methods of fundraising for capital-intensive projects.

In a sense, crowdfunding has made innovation more accessible. In a similar way to the democratization of opinion that has occurred with social media, crowdfunding has helped democratize access to capital, and thereby, innovation.

Crowdfunding began as **donation-based**, based mainly on the goodwill of backers who have a passionate connection to the founder's aim, usually related to a social cause or charity. More recently, **rewards-based** crowdfunding has become a major source of funding for product developers, authors, artists, and others trying to raise funds. In return for a certain level of investment, an investor becomes eligible for a reward, the value of which may increase as the level of investment increases. The two biggest crowdfunding platforms, Kickstarter and Indiegogo, offer both rewards and donation based funding.

A third model of crowdfunding is emerging that could dramatically change the funding landscape even further: **equity-based** crowdfunding. In this form of financing, entrepreneurs use portals online portals regulated by the SEC and FINRA to get access to a large pool of investors to whom they can sell non-voting shares of their startup.

Crowdfunding is a truly innovative model of financing in itself, one that also helps foster innovation at the grassroots. Crowdfunding is no joke, with potential to launch startups into the upper echelons. In 2012, Oculus Rift, a virtual-reality gaming headset, raised $2.4 million via crowdfunding. Just two years later, it was acquired by Facebook for $2 billion.

But the significance of crowdfunding is not limited to startups taking moonshots. Crowdfunding has been a driver of innovation mostly at a smaller scale. The bulk of innovation being supported by crowdfunding exists in the domain of artists, authors, entrepreneurs, and even communities.

For my previous book, *Mobile Ready*, I was in talks with publishing houses, but nothing about the deals they were offering appealed to me. In the end, my entrepreneurial spirit took over and I decided to self-publish. As part of this strategy, I decided to crowdfund the publication of my book. Using a site named Publishizer, I set a goal of $10,000 to fund the book. Although I chose this route mainly for the learning experience, it worked out extremely well, with my campaign pulling in $18,000.

I was sold on the potential of crowdfunding to not just provide a source of funding for entrepreneurial endeavors, but to connect entrepreneurs with audiences—and as we'll talk about in a moment, allow them to co-create their products and services with those audiences.

Crowdfunding is helping to upend the dominance and concentration of venture capital in facilitating innovation. Most venture capital is currently concentrated in two parts of the country: Silicon Valley and Boston. One study showed that from 2009 to 2015, 50 percent of all venture capital dollars were concentrated in just four counties in these two metro areas.

But in looking at crowdfunding, "The study found that crowdfunding in a region, and in particular successful technology campaigns, appeared to cause an increase in venture capital funding in the region."

The Huge Upside of Crowdfunding

So why exactly has crowdfunding taken off to such a degree? There are several reasons it is such an attractive financing model.

For starters, crowdfunding is a great way to reduce the inherent risk in new product development and manufacturing. One of the constraints of the major crowdfunding platforms is that the entrepreneur must set a specific funding goal—a dollar number at which they will be able to execute a profitable product launch, setting the expectation among the product's backers that the product will not come to market unless the goal is reached. This provides risk reduction, because the founder is not on the hook for delivering the product, or any additional promised rewards, if the funding goal is not met. The risk of this model is that the time, energy, and resources spent on a crowdfunding campaign may be wasted—if the funding goal is not met, the founder will not received any of the pledged money. It's all or nothing.

Second, crowdfunding also increases freedom to build innovative solutions. It reduces reliance on banks, private investors and government grants—risk-averse sources of funding, especially when it comes to the largest institutions. Startups and individuals can take creative gambles that they would not have been able to do through traditional methods of financing.

Third, crowdfunding is not only a source of funds—it's also a source of valuable information: feedback that can help founders improve a product or service. By facilitating intimate access to the voice of the customer, crowdfunding is a highly effective mechanism to practice objective customer empathy.

Project backers tend to be eager early adopters, so they are excited to provide feedback. They can also be great "evangelists" for it, spreading awareness of the product to other potential customers.

Research by MIT Sloan found that "campaigns attract fewer backers when most of the product development activities are completed before crowdfunding." The more objectively customer empathetic a campaign is—the more it incorporates the voice of the customer into the *product development* process—the more successful it is.

And even an unsuccessful campaign (one that doesn't hit its funding goal) could be deemed a success if the market feedback it provides helps improve a later iteration of the product or opens the founders' eyes to a new direction to tackle.

Crowdfunding does have its downsides. Managing a marketing campaign, all while analyzing and incorporating the product feedback from backers, can be time and resource consuming, especially for an individual or small organization.

Crowdfunding is still emerging as a competitive tool in the corporate innovation arsenal, but watch it closing over the coming years as more companies look to leverage the power of pre-demand funding for new products and services.

PART 3

LOOKING FORWARD: THE ROADMAP TO THE FUTURE

Chapter 10
PROGRESSIVE COMPANIES AND
THEIR ARMIES OF DIGITAL NATIVES

They are everywhere. The teenage girl listening to music via iPhone on the train. The new office recruit who knows exactly how to fix your PC when it crashes. Your twenty-something son who prefers Netflix to CBS. They are "digital natives" and they are everywhere.

The term originated in a 2001 article entitled "Digital Natives, Digital Immigrants" by education consultant Marc Prensky, but has moved well beyond the scope of education to be widely used in business as well as popular culture. A digital native is someone born after 1980, who grew up with the rise of social media, which began embryonically with Usenet, and online forums, and today is epitomized by the likes of Facebook and Twitter.

While it's possible to argue the term itself is painting with a broad brush, and that the digital savvy generation actually began with the previous generation— those who created the basis of the technology now so widespread, the difference from an innovation and business perspective is these "kids" are connected. They connect socially in different ways using the vast array of technology available online and through mobile apps, and it's this connection, this community, that as a group make them powerful, and this is what makes them an "army." Progressive companies realize this.

Digital natives are obviously the segment in the market that most organizations have the biggest gap in terms of understanding, so it's important to have people internally that can help to close that gap in understanding that market segment. Often digital natives are different enough and they inspire enough curiosity that corporate managers will hire a person basically because they understand Snapchat, or simply because think differently. And that's not a bad thing. It can be positive in the sense that it's basically saying: how are digital natives thinking differently than me—how can they challenge me? These digital natives, particularly ones that come through management training programs will often be accelerated through the hierarchy to have senior executive exposure, not necessarily because they're amazing talent, simply because they possess useful insight into their own market. It's an illustration of just how important it's become for brands to be able to speak to, to develop technology, and products that fit the needs of digital natives.

Social media today plays a huge role in how brands build trust in a digital marketplace. A brand's word is its bond, and digital natives can keep companies accountable if they break their promises. Reviews, forums, Facebook, Twitter are all platforms for feedback, which are readily accessible and widely used by digital natives. Some companies do this better than others and the tactics used by progressive companies for creating and maintaining trust offer models for other companies attempting to connect with consumers in new channels and in unique ways. The big boys—the Doves, the Oreos, the Red Bulls all do it very well—engaging consumers at all levels. The big successes though are the disruptive innovation companies such as Airbnb, Uber, Snapchat, and Netflix that have made a strategy out of connecting, and provide a blueprint for how brands, large and small, that did (or did not) begin in the digital age—can grow. A progressive company engages digital natives on their terms.

While online feedback outlets are not new concepts, what progressive companies do is to integrate social media as an integral part of feedback for their brands and create entirely new models on which to build reputation and trust through armies of digital natives.

The lesson is, these armies are allies you want on your side.

How Technology has Created Armies of Digital Natives

We all have to accept the clear and absolute truth; the advancement of consumer technology and the internet has shifted the balance of power from the company to the user/consumer. The "connected and information empowered" consumer has significant impact on brand perception, product acceptance, and adoption models, when compared to say the 1980s. Consumers today expect and easily await the next big thing from companies, and if it fails to meet their expectations they are pretty vocal in expressing their displeasure over social networks.

How many times have you personally clicked "like" or shared a complaint about a product or service? How many times have you seen mainstream media pick up on a bad-experience consumer story, simply because an unhappy customer created a particularly poignant or funny story about it on social media? Just as an army of digital natives behind you can promote your brand, so they can equality tarnish it. You could simply blame online sharing, but you just have yourself to blame if you're not actively trying to incorporate reliable two-way feedback systems within your own social media.

Today, the need for companies to listen to the consumer, and to work together to meet market needs, and solve problems is a vital part of building successful businesses and products. A large number of companies have suffered or vanished due to a disconnect with their market: Blockbuster, Kodak, Borders to name a few.

Something else companies need to keep in mind—that's often impossible to anticipate in isolation—is the way technology has ushered in a set of new accepted behaviors in society. In the late 1990s the vast majority of people were convinced they would never get a cellphone—because who would want to be connected and available 24/7? Similarly, circa 2009, many people swore they'd never join Facebook, because they just couldn't see the point, yet as of 2016 the total number of active Facebook users worldwide amounts to 2.2 billion (Statisca).

Technology isn't the only innovative force driving change. So too are the consumers that use the technology in ways never envisioned by the manufacturer. For example, the popularity of selfies, or food photos, or planking (for that matter) were certainly not anticipated by the inventors of cellphone cameras. It seemed like a cool add-on to the mobile device at the time, but the ease of using the phone camera combined with social media popularity led to the explosion of all kinds of photos being posted online. That new behavior then spawned a whole new market of software applications (e.g. advanced photo sharing and filtering apps like Instagram) and consumer goods (e.g. selfie sticks) that likely never would have existed had it not been for the swelling force of innovation nurtured by digital natives.

Such behavior conditioning has powerful economic implications. Consumers use technology in new ways to facilitate purchases with greater ease, mobility, and velocity.

Digital Natives Raise the Bar for Established Companies

Established companies may not be doing enough, or may simply not be able to do enough to change and restructure themselves to face the trials of future competitive innovation. Start-ups can enter what were assumed to be restricted markets and make huge inroads that ultimately cut into the profits of corporate giants. It's partly the result of equality or level playing field that technology provides, but it's also a result of culture. Established companies have a "this is how it's always been done attitude." A new start-up like Airbnb has no such baggage and isn't limited by the ways of the past.

The lesson here is that brands have to integrate their experience so it's the same in-store, online, and on mobile devices. Consumers want the luxury of being able to make purchases anyhow, anywhere, which means that companies and organizations have to be far more innovative in their methods of communicating with their customers. How many companies would have actively maintained social media even five years ago? A handful. Today it's not just a matter of having a Facebook and Twitter account and updating them daily, companies need to share their brand experience with customers *daily*.

Digitally savvy customers are no longer a niche market: they are the main market. Social media empowers them to take their entire network with them, 24 hours a day, 7 days a week—providing a means for individuals to connect, collaborate, rally, and produce beyond traditional boundaries.

To truly connect with digital natives **multichannel retailing** or **omnichannel retailing** is necessary to provide a variety of channels in a customer's shopping experience. Mobile computing, triggered by the launch of the iPhone in June 2007, has become the universal enabler of ecosystems that travel with us as we experience life and the world around us. Vast numbers of customers pre-shop before even entering a store. Because of this customers are often more versed in product specs than frontline staff. In the past it's been common for customers to do that pre-shopping online but then prefer to make a purchase in the retail store. The smartphone experience shows that trend changing. You'll find digital natives pre-shopping in-store, checking deals on an online store on a smartphone, while looking at reviews on social networks or asking their friends for recommendations via social network, and will make the purchase online with their phone as they walk out of the store.

As a market force, digital armies are beginning to have tremendous influence not only on what technology products get made and how they are used but also on how the companies that make that technology are structured. The very core of such companies—their organizational design—is being altered to ensure that they are imbued with the right characteristics, functions, and business models to support the growing demands of digital natives. For example, you'll find shoppers favor retailers that offer a total experience. Multichannel retailers will have the biggest clout, supporting customers to shop in-store, online, and on mobile platforms. Retailers need to find ways to engage with these customers at different stages of their path to purchase. At the simplest, it's providing recommendations on checkout, making sure all the relevant product specifications are at their fingertips, offering instant online chat, but also in providing a personal experience across online and offline channels.

At a certain point in their lifecycle, the challenge for companies seeking relevance and growth shifts from addressing the needs of digital natives and becomes the cause of activating their digital native consumer base as a consolidated and concentrated force—an army—that can lead the charge for further product adoption and innovation.

How Progressive Companies Activate Armies of Digital Natives

Progressive companies will be the organizations that see armies of digital natives as an ally, and seek for ways to deploy those armies on their own behalf. They will engage their users as frequently as possible, giving them an experience that they want to tell their network about—and you can better believe they will tell everyone they know via their myriad social media channels, especially if the experience is negative. Progressive companies are also realizing that no longer can you design a product or service in isolation to fit your market.

There are two opposing approaches to developing design and interface for this new world of digital natives: User-centered design (UCD) and user-led design (ULD).

User-centered design (UCD) is a process in which the needs, and wants, of end users of a product or service are given broad attention at each stage of the design process. The innovative ideas and resulting products will still be driven by the company employees.

User-led design (ULD) on the other hand is characterized by the concept that users are often best placed to identify their own needs and supply the best ideas about ways to meet them, with company employees playing roles as orchestrators and facilitators.

Both are a far cry from the **traditional approach** to product design which has generally been an in-house process where employees developed ideas and products, and then focus groups of potential customers were canvassed to find out their perceptions. Real market feedback wouldn't actually come until the product was ready for market. I'm not saying that in-house innovation doesn't work. It was at the forefront of innovative business practices for the best part of a century. Steve Jobs was famous for not asking consumers, but rather giving the customer what they want. "It's really hard to design products by focus groups. A lot of times, people don't know what they want until you show it to them," Jobs told *BusinessWeek* in 1998. This has been the approach of Apple and many other companies and, let's be honest, it's served them well until now.

What we have now today with UCD and ULD is companies recognizing that the process of product creation should be one of co-creating with the market.

Which approach is better? Both ULD and UCD involve the customer, in the process; they vary only in the weight and timing of that involvement. Both are arrows to the future, and a growing trend of getting digital natives on-board early on in the product development process.

Where user centered design beats out user led design, is in those cases where the customer doesn't know yet what they want. Henry Ford's famous quote on the subject of the introduction of the automobile to the consumer market is of course, "If I had asked people what they wanted, they would have said faster horses." Being user centered therefore sometimes involves ignoring, or even going against customer desires in order to better serve the customer. We'll talk more about this in later chapters, but user centered is focusing on the problem, rather than being fixed on a single solution. When you're first looking at a problem, you want to get deep into the problem, involving your customers, your allies, your digital natives, without being distracted by, or deciding on solutions they (or you) may initially come up with. You want to understand the pain of the problem, and this will often lead to the design of a far better solution than anyone may have initially come up with. It's all about building the best possible product to solve the customer's problem, as opposed to coming up with the best possible product.

By doing this, progressive companies are gaining an empathetic understanding of what the product is trying to achieve, as well as looking deeply at behaviors that the market is already demonstrating, along the way engaging digital natives and asking what is the value proposition of what we're doing? What is the product's positioning? What else is involved in the value chain? By clarifying these things early on it's easier to join the dots in terms of building a successful product that the market wants versus an isolated one that it doesn't.

The other benefit to early customer involvement in innovation is that it can be a lot quicker. The previous process involved pilots and proof-of-concept testing with focus groups, and until these occurred much was unknown. How well would the consumer take to the new product? Would they even like it? It was a very slow process that could unfold over several years. Involving the consumer much earlier means you've already got a pretty good idea of what they like and don't. You aren't for example going to be blown away by customer apathy to a new product, like Ford was when despite a $400 million development budget, they introduced the customer sight unseen Edsel back in 1957.

Anyway, today the process can't be slow. There's much pressure to innovate. Customers want the next big thing. Sooner rather than later. Expectations are high. It has to be great. Today a "test and learn" approach is becoming more popular with companies trying new things and getting feedback quickly so they can in turn respond. These initiatives can foster brand loyalty by making customers feel important, empowered and emotionally connected to the brand, and before you know it, your digital army is assembling.

Remember Myspace? Hi5? Friendster? It's actually been over a decade since businesses became actively involved in the process of trying to communicate to consumers via social media. Social media platforms have come, then vanished. Today there's been a dramatic shift in the way companies communicate globally with audiences. Social media evolved in a bit of a hit and miss process and so it's been with corporate attempts to utilize it in the most effective way. Also, social media isn't fixed, it's static. So if for instance the market shifts to Snapchat, you need to move away from Facebook to Snapchat. Maybe it'll then move to YO or something else; whatever happens you need to engage digital natives on their terms.

No longer seen as a distraction—social media has widely impacted organizations across all areas not just marketing, communications, and customer service. Where "scalable" was once the buzzword—reaching as many potential customers through social media as possible—today it's recognized that social media's strengths are relationship building, networking, and customer service. Companies really need to get personal.

Today, social strategists focus their efforts on integrating with broader digital initiatives such as content strategy and using social data for better informed decision-making. Yet it's a particularly complex process to integrate rapidly changing social platforms (like Facebook and Twitter) into the complex digital business environment. The big guys don't have it all easy. The larger the organization, the larger the challenge. "You can imagine the complexity of managing a global brand that spans 119 countries with thousands of franchise-owned restaurants focused on local market needs," Global director of social at

McDonald's Matthew Tennant says. "Analytics can be foundational to managing social's opportunities and risks at scale."

As well as facilitating active social media engagement, passive social listening can also provide companies with a feeling for what customers like and don't like about their products. Simply listening online to social media, forums and communities can aid a company in their innovation projects.

Companies have made large inroads with social media programs that focus on customer service, events, and sponsorship. These work for a number of reasons. They focus on the main benefit of social media: relationship-building. Also on the whole these relationship-building strategies are programs that are natural extensions of existing business practices. For example, customer service via social media is an extension of a department's objectives, just as adding website help and email support has been in the past. What comes next? Social media platforms with fully integrated customer relationship management (CRM) or sales departments?

So just how do companies do it? How do they harness the power of digital natives and become progressive? It is not impossible, but it does take a combination of creativity and risk. Let's take a closer look at the case studies of two progressive companies and how they have changed consumer behavior through innovation.

IKEA: Innovating Through User-Centered Design

You explore IKEA's New Innovation Lab in Copenhagen. There are prototypes, new design ideas; the expected sleek, simple furniture, and other household items which seem unusual and unknown. A table that turns heat into electricity and charges your phones, an art piece that only appears on the wall when your household energy consumption reduces; these are just a few examples of what you will find here in Space 10. The public come in, stroll around, see what the future may hold and offer feedback.

Space 10's mission is investigating the future of modern living and design through a series of collaborative labs. Each lab sets out to tackle a specific challenge, through seminars, workshops, pitches, residencies, exhibitions, and other joint projects with designers, artists, and creatives from around the world. Space 10 is located in trendy—arguably the home of design—Copenhagen. Although entirely funded by IKEA, Space 10 is completely independent. The day-to-day operations are handled by a small Danish design firm, Rebel Agency.

What IKEA gets is the first look at all the new concepts that come out of it. These are not design ideas that you'll see in IKEA's 2017 catalogue, but ideas which might eventually disrupt their business—and be in their entirely different 2027 catalogue.

It is the definition of innovation and shouldn't be surprising coming from a company that changed the furniture business model along with the behavior of its consumers.

Founder Ingvar Kamprad started young. Incredible though it is to believe, Kamprad was just seventeen when he started the business that would bear his initials (I.K.) along with the first letters of Elmtaryd and Agunnaryd, the farm and village where he grew up. Initially IKEA sold pencils.

There is a long list of innovative concepts, well beyond gimmicks, when it comes to IKEA: nicely designed furniture at low cost, a café and restaurant in-store, a furniture catalogue, stores located in suburbs as destination shopping, and shopping as a lifestyle event. Innovation has become an ingrained part of IKEA's culture.

But the big innovation idea that defines IKEA is the showroom alongside the flat-pack warehouse. No one had tried it before. Or even thought of it. Who would even imagine it would work? Yet Kamprad believed people would enjoy assembling their own furniture so long as it came with detailed instructions. Shipping flat-packs also significantly reduced shipping costs. The idea changed the behavior of consumers.

The apocryphal story according to a 2013 IKEA press release is the idea of flat-pack furniture came from designer Gillis Lundgren (who was the fourth employee for IKEA). A LOVET table was being used in an IKEA catalogue photography session but its three-legged, leaf shape proved too cumbersome for Lundgren to fit into the car. To solve this, he removed the legs and, that sparked the flat-pack, self-assembly revolution. It did a number of things.

- It instantly made IKEA products cheaper as the customers did the assembling.
- Shipping costs were slashed because the company's products are flat.
- IKEA could keep more product in stock in the warehouse since only the showroom pieces required to be assembled.
- It led the way for furniture designers to create clean, functional furnishings, defining the Scandinavian design along the way.
- It took away the delivery problem for larger items—customers could now fit almost any furniture item into a family car.

Not only is IKEA's flat-pack folklore a brilliant spark of innovation that solved an immediate need (fitting the LOVET table in Lundgren's car) it also addressed an urgent consumer need (getting larger items home). The innovation occurred within the landscape of use—the consumer using the product out in the world. By channeling that perspective into their product design at a systemic level, IKEA has institutionalized the practice of seeing their products through the eyes of their consumer base and rewarding them by engineering products to match their consumer behaviors. Such innovation, or any form of innovation really, requires constraints. The constraint of physical space afforded the epiphany showcased here.

Flat-packing was a moment of innovation that became integral to the IKEA "concept" and the company was able to recognize and capitalize on it in such fundamental way that it continues to delight and reward customers today.

Innovative? Well yeah. Think about it: before this, you would walk into a showroom, pick out a table or couch you wanted and the company would then arrange delivery of it (usually on a Tuesday or Friday or other set delivery day that suited them). IKEA changed the whole purchasing and delivery process. You walk through the vast design-display areas, select your product, then head to the warehouse and pick up the kitset. As such it will likely fit in your car. Then you spend an afternoon (doing your best to) assemble it.

Europeans in particular liked the idea because it made products much easier to purchase and travel with on public transport unassembled. With barely the blink of an eye, the largest change to date in furniture delivery had taken place.

Although IKEA may be a giant retailer, it's managed to create a brand image that's both practical and homely and customers feel part of. A great part of that is they can own, paint, stain, assemble, and have their own hand in the furniture they purchase.

The flat-pack innovation is even more relevant today for reasons unforeseen when it was introduced by IKEA back in 1956: the corporate carbon footprint. "We hate waste," says IKEA CEO Mikael Ohlsson, who gives the example of the popular three-seater "Ektorp" sofa—which his designers managed to find a way to pack more compactly, doubling the amount of sofa they could fit into a given volume of space. That took €100 ($135) from the price tag—while also dramatically reducing the carbon-dioxide emissions involved in transport and delivery.

IKEA is one of the rare companies which have innovation at its bedrock philosophy. Today there's an IKEA app that enables users to visualize in real time how furniture items would look in their own room. It just might be one of the most innovative ways for IKEA to establish its digital army allies: the app will only facilitate more engagement with IKEA customers, and as a result engender more of their allegiance.

Direct consumer engagement through digital technologies is proving to be a common denominator for today's most innovative companies. The mobile phone is the platform of choice. IKEA is far from alone in terms of exploiting the direct access into consumers' hands and minds that such a platform provides. Airbnb is another progressive company disrupting a major industry—hospitality—by empowering (and delighting) its consumers with mobilized capabilities. And by democratizing the marketplace, they've disrupted their industry to a whole new level.

Airbnb: Innovating Through User-Led Design

San Francisco, October 2007. The Industrial Design Conference held by Industrial Designers Society of America. Two designers—college friends, Joe Gebbia and Brian Chesky—talk about their love of design icons Charles and Ray

Eames—well known for their development of modern architecture and furniture but also influential in the fields of industrial and graphic design. They decide that a simple, clean design ascetic must be a part the new business venture they have conceived.

Earlier in the week Gebbia calls Chesky and offers him a room. Chesky impulsively quits his job and drives to San Francisco with a foam mattress in the back of his car. It never occurs to him until arriving that he can't afford to pay rent.

That weekend because of the conference all the hotels are sold out. They immediately hit upon an idea: *"Why don't we make our apartment into a little bed and breakfast?"*

That weekend they make more than $1,000 hosting three visitors from the conference, and find they love having guests to show around the city. As a bonus they don't end up homeless.

Gebbia and Chesky wonder what would happen if other people like them—people who could use some extra cash and have an extra room or air mattress—had access to a marketplace where they could list their lodging accommodations, set their pricing and availability, and welcome paying guests as often as they like. A new business model is born.

The two quickly build a website originally called Airbedandbreakfast.com, pitch investors, and promote the concept on blogs and by telling "everyone we knew," according to Chesky.

As of 2017 Airbnb is a company valued at $31 billion (Marketwatch).

Soon after Airbnb's launch came the 2008 Democratic National Convention. Hotels in Denver quickly sold out, and along came a thousand listings on Airbnb.com to help fill that accommodation gap. It confirmed for Gebbia and Chesky that the market potential was huge. Part of the success is actually very simple: Airbnb fulfilled a need for short term accommodation. Hotels have limited space available and rooms can sell out at peak time or during special events. Many home and apartment owners have a spare room doing little beyond junk storage. Innovation is about solving customer problems.

It's also a blueprint for the new **Network Orchestrators** business model. This blueprint applies not only to Airbnb, but also YouTube, Wikipedia, BlaBlaCar,

Upwork… the list goes on. Yet to the hotel industry Airbnb appeared to come out of nowhere. The hotel industry was trapped by their past success and unable to conceive of a company that could come along and take the (already existing) bed and breakfast market and turn it into threat that could dramatically impact its business.

The Harvard Business Review defines four business models. They are:

- *Asset Builders:* These companies make, market, distribute, and sell physical things. Examples include the Ford Motor Company, Abercrombie & Fitch, and Apple.
- *Service Providers:* These companies provide services to customers. Examples include AOL, American Express, and JP Morgan.
- *Technology Creators:* These companies trade in intellectual property such as software, pharmaceuticals, and biotechnology. Examples include Microsoft, Oracle, and Google.

These first three could be seen as largely following the traditional business model. The fourth has tended to disrupt many of the traditional models in various industries over the past decade.

Network Orchestrators. These companies create a network of peers in which the users cooperate and share in the value creation. Examples include eBay, Airbnb, Grab, Uber, Tripadvisor, and Alibaba.

Network Orchestrators like Airbnb have these key attributes in common.

1. **Rethinks value creation:** Network Orchestrators allow anyone with the required asset (a car, a room) to become a provider by giving them access and tools (website) to market themselves to a potentially global market.
2. **Rethinks value consumption:** It wasn't unheard of, but was uncommon for travelers to rideshare or stay at strangers' apartments. Network Orchestrators create a new consumer behavior.
3. **Rethinks quality control:** Hotels (and motels) are known for quality and good customer service. Traditional taxis are safe. Network Orchestrators

on the other hand, rely on a peer rating and reporting function to ensure quality, safety and reliability.

4. **Rethinks scale:** A traditional business scales by adding more capacity through new properties or fleet. Network Orchestrators don't own inventory. Instead they scale by improving ability to match users and leverage vast quantities or better data.

Airbnb and other Network Orchestrators take advantage of not requiring growth by investment to build physical infrastructure. They don't need great pools of property and assets. They provide a marketplace of suppliers and consumers, merely clipping the ticket on all transactions. By doing so they can create markets that didn't exist before and can grow these markets into millions, if not billions, of participants.

Airbnb focuses on creating customer driven value—by peer-to-peer review and recommendation. Hotel chains can only dream of having access to strategic data, the likes of which Airbnb generates, to guide their business model and provide more services for clients. It goes far beyond what customers are spending on each room and where they stay. Airbnb knows the full profile of the traveler, the full details of all their traveling preferences, and can target customers with accurate and specific offers.

Thanks to social media and the sheer widespread adoption of smartphones companies can now much more quickly and easily, ask for, and receive feedback on products during the idea generation and design stages, rather than simply during product testing. This creates a far more collaborative environment and reduces the risk that products will either underperform or fail totally. It's an environment where information can be shared and insights provided in real time across social and other networks.

Times change, and innovation is becoming a cut-throat battle ground in every industry. Companies are under increased pressure to innovate and this is leading them to involve the consumer much earlier in the product development lifecycle than they ever have in the past.

If companies are going to remain relevant, they need to find ways to incorporate the growing ranks of digital natives into their innovation strategy, whether through designing products and experiences with the user squarely in mind, as IKEA has done, or pivoting to become facilitators of a service model that allows users to create value directly, à la Airbnb.

Chapter 11

THE FACTORIES OF SELF-DISRUPTION: INNOVATION LABS AND VENTURE TEAMS

T rue innovation requires a paradigm shift. In the 1900s, the steam locomotive was king, and businesses that built them were some of the most common startups of the era. Then the automobile came along, and swept the rug out from under the old order. The companies that survived were those that recognized that the automobile's arrival meant they could no longer be in the *locomotive* business—they were now in the *transportation* business. And transportation meant that the locomotive was only one possible solution. They could also produce a car, or an airplane. The companies that kept going realized their core competency and mission in life was not in locomotives, but locomotion.

A modern-day example can be seen with the insurance sector. A lot of health and life insurance companies will tell you that their core mission is to be a health and life insurance company. But if you look under the bonnet, they're far more profitable the longer someone lives and the healthier they are. So if you have a healthier-than-normal lifestyle and exceed life expectancy, then you are more profitable for your insurance company. This suggests that the commercial alignment of the insurance company should be to the elongation and improvement of one's quality of life. This makes these companies not health and life insurance companies, but rather *health and life* companies.

These are both simple reframes, at least apparently, but ones with potentially massive ramifications. In the case of the insurance company, this reframe may lead the company to decide that insurance per se may not be the only solution it wants to offer; perhaps it will get into preventative or proactive measures like promoting exercise and other lifestyle interventions that improve the quality of life of the policyholder and the long-term profitability of the insurance product.

It's a shift in the company's mindset and purpose, one that allows them to explore the exact same problem set as before, but from a totally different perspective. This same phenomenon is occurring in other sectors too right now, including education, financial services, and harkening to the disruptive 1900s, even transportation. By challenging the value proposition, and the purpose of transportation, Uber has disrupted an entire industry.

What these examples show is that innovation can flourish when companies are willing to *disrupt themselves*—to question their identity and business model in some way, or to at least create a space in which alternative identities and models can be explored. The standout examples of companies like Apple, Google, IKEA, and Airbnb aside, there are frameworks available to today's organizations that want to enable disruption and innovation, either directly within their own ranks or through targeted outside ventures.

Let's look at two of the biggest examples of these frameworks.

Innovation Labs

Innovation labs are the first way progressive companies are seeking to incorporate innovation into their culture. An innovation lab generally consists of a small cell within a company or just outside the company, one with enough separation from the traditional structure of the main organization that it can pursue innovative ideas the larger organization may not wish to pursue.

Numerous multinationals are setting up innovation labs or innovation teams in multiple countries in attempts to catch up to the Airbnbs, Ubers, Googles, and Apples of the world. These labs vary in their investments, goals, and commitments, but they all represent a spirit of experimentation outside the bounds of the parent organization's business-as-usual function. These progressive companies often recruit and hire digital natives to form the backbone of their innovation labs, which serve as internal think tanks to listen to vocal users on social channels and observe leading edge market forces.

Dedicated innovation functions via innovation labs represent an attempt to bring a culture of innovation to an organization, and in time, even a very small cell can have a culture-changing effect. Rather than trying to change the entire organization, it's easier to start with a small team of 20 people that can follow its own path. Innovation labs provide a setting in which to experiment with how a company could operate differently. In many cases, the innovation lab aims to exemplify how the whole organization could and should behave, also knowing that this shift needs to start small; it takes time and patience to turn the cultural Titanic of a large, well-established organization.

I've spent the last couple of years building the innovation lab at US insurance company MetLife, and helping AIA explore strategic options in the health and life space, working with Norwegian Telco Group Telenor as it aims to build innovative culture across its markets, or Malaysian media giant pursue aspirations of transforming their organisation. The banking sector also employs innovation labs, particularly to address challenges related to changes in the financial income system. Unilever has a big lab in Singapore called the Foundry, which focuses on exploring new consumer needs, particularly those around new market sensitivities. You don't have to dig too far to find examples.

There are many different flavors of innovation lab: everything from a full-scale lab that involves participation with the startup ecosystem in the parent company's industry, to full research and development facilities, to learning facilities, to cultural development facilities. Each serves different purposes, depending on the organization's objective. The types of innovation labs can be summarized broadly into three categories:

The "Look Good" category. Companies that set up innovation programs to *look* innovative. They're never going to do anything, but they look cool. They're usually the ones that buy very expensive furniture, install art pieces and high-tech gadgets like VR screens to wow people—but it's usually all image, or what you might call "innovation theater." These companies are not creating a foundation for cultivating innovation because they misunderstand what innovation is about: shiny toys and looking innovative, rather than embracing the cultural and operating perspectives that will drive true innovation. This model may sound negative, but it plays an important purpose for many companies. For a publicly listed company, looking innovative is good PR, which has increased shareholder value—so even this false image can play a positive role. But it's ultimately just innovation window dressing. The analogy is they went out and bought a new suit. They look good, but will ditch that look when something new is fashionable and hot.

The "Feel Good" category. This category is more internally focused around culture and people, and making the internal environment *feel* innovative. It typically involves things like workshops, internal hackathons, and attempts to change the way they work internally. There's often mixed results with this model, with both failures and great successes. While this is a valuable starting point for enabling innovation, the danger lies in only inspiring employees to be innovative, but not giving them the means to execute those ideas effectively. This can actually drive employees away, potentially leaving the organization out of frustration and to pursue their ideas elsewhere.

In a way, the "Feel Good" category is the inverse of the "Look Innovative" category, which is focused on PR value and the public's perception of the organization. "Feel Good" is usually driven from a Head of Innovation working in conjunction with someone in HR, or Learning, or Cultural Development.

The "Feel Good" category comes closer to true innovation than the "Look Good" category, but both categories have their limitations. Whether a company remains stuck in one of these categories is not set in stone. They stay in this phase is state-based, but the feel good ones are a little bit different because "feel good" will inspire the employer base to want to do something. The problem with this is if you suddenly inspire your employees to want to do something but then never allow anyone to do anything substantial, you can actually create a distance within the employee. The worst thing you want to do is incentivize employees to find innovative ideas but then give them no capability to actually execute the ideas, because then they're likely to leave and work on those ideas outside your company or for another company.

The "Do Innovation" category. This incorporates the elements of both the "Look Good" and "Feel Good" categories, where not only are companies externally collaborating with startups and building spaces and so forth, but they are also encouraging and enabling their internal workforce to think and act differently, and to pursue either adjacent or completely disruptive paths for the organization. This category is the aspirational form of innovation experimentation; it's the hardest to achieve, but also the one from which the most meaningful innovation can emerge.

The execution of ideas could simply be to improve on the current business, known as incremental innovation. Or it can aspire to create a portfolio of strategic options to transform the business, otherwise known as disruptive innovation.

Venture Teams

Another way that companies seek innovation is through venture teams, groups within a company that seek to create an innovative portfolio of investments, compared to an innovation lab, which is more hands on with customer research and carrying out actual innovation.

These two competencies, innovation labs and venture teams, are different but complementary. While innovations labs focuses on internal innovation, venture teams focus on innovation by association. An innovation team technically is agnostic of the ideas they're working on. Their function rests more on the culture and capability side, aiming to become like a pipeline for ideas. A venture team is interested in investing in successful ideas. Both, however, involve risk. And both venture teams and innovation labs value ideas in similar ways, by evaluating them using on a return-on-capital model. In other words, if you have a venture team and an innovation team in the same company, they should be working off the same valuation models.

A venture team might spend $50,000 on an internal company idea, valuing it as though it were a startup in its portfolio, in the same way a venture firm would look at a company in its investment portfolio. The venture team would ask the same kinds of questions a venture firm might about its investment: Do we expand on it? Do we diversify? Do we change the problem set it's looking at? Do we kill it?

A lot of companies' strategies include a venture division whose job it is to make investments that improve the financial performance of the organization. But what we're seeing today is a lot more established companies investing in startups with the potential to disrupt the industry of the established company. Hypothetically, Harvard might invest in Coursera, or T-mobile might invest in some new communication startup. The larger company acts as an investor knowing they don't have time (or inclination) to do the innovation themselves, but they're happy to give these start-up companies the resources they need to fuel the fire—and in so doing, potentially unseating the status quo in their own domain. Interesting times.

A decade of constant digital disruption has left most industries vulnerable. Mature, unchanging systems, processes and structure limit the capabilities and culture of multinational companies. The challenge is tough for most incumbent companies, as their success is their limitation. They've amassed decades of lessons that have narrowed their view on success, and more importantly their risk appetite.

At the same time, the siren call of innovation is strong. Innovation is a concept with cachet, and unfortunately this means that many companies use innovation as another notch in their belt, an optics play, rather than an endeavor to create something new and disruptive. Companies can either look good, feel good, or do good when it comes to innovation—or they attempt to attain the holy grail and practice all three together.

Whether through a venture team or an innovation lab, organizations have different models at their disposal to achieve innovation in action. So those are the operating models—but where's the handbook? How does a company get started creating the groundwork, culture, and processes that will allow innovation to flourish through their own innovation lab or venture team? Precisely how they can do that is the central question, and it's what the rest of this book will answer.

Chapter 12
CONTEXT—HOW INNOVATION WARS START

Nothing occurs in a vacuum—and that's certainly the case with innovation. Innovation is the key to financial success, which is why so many companies, organizations, and governments around the world are looking to improve their innovation efforts. But many companies find themselves stuck performing innovation theater—locked into the "Look Good" or "Feel Good" stages of innovation I outlined in the previous chapter, and unsure of how to create the rigorous environment and conditions for true innovation to unfold.

A quick scan of the bookshelves or the Internet will reveal a lot of recipes out there for unshackling a company's innovation potential. What I'm about to discuss in these next nine chapters is my personal recipe for success with innovation, one I term the *4Cs and 4Ps of Innovation*. Listed here for the first time in this form, these reflect my personal strategy for innovation success based upon my own observation and experience throughout my fifteen-year-plus career in the innovation trenches.

The 4Cs and 4Ps represent two overlapping strategies. The 4Cs reflect what an *organization* needs to do to be innovative, while the 4Ps are what an innovative *individual* requires. Each is meant to serve as one of the components in a complex but complete strategy for success. For an organization or individual, possessing just one, two, or even three of these elements isn't enough. For this strategy to claim victory, then all these diverse components need to work in synergy.

We'll cover the 4Cs of innovation success at the organizational level first. They are:

- Context
- Culture
- Capability
- Collaboration

Let's break each of these elements down, starting with Context.

Context

When I began working seriously with innovations programs, I often found they would get off the ground, and they'd get great internal support—but they would lose momentum along the way, or wouldn't make it past key checkpoints in the innovation process. Often, the organization wouldn't invest more than a few thousand dollars in experiments, and as a result, projects and ideas weren't evolving and expanding as they needed to.

What was missing was a solid foundation. You can start really innovative projects, and create a bunch of seedlings, but without context, none of those seedlings will grow into an orchard. What I realized in my experience with these organizations is that there's no point ploughing a field if the soil is bad from the start. You need to have fertilized soil; you need to have chosen the right place, along with the right climate.

I define *Context* as everything to do with the structure of an organization: the financial incentives, the hierarchy, the property you build—the foundation that allows innovation to either flourish or fail. This also includes your strategic horizons. How well do you understand your current situation, such as strengths, weaknesses, opportunities and of course threats. This links to a future aspirational goal of the purpose and value you will create for customers in the future, typically five years (independent of product and services). It's easier to build from the ground up if you're a startup, but context is equally important if you're an established company, to make sure you have the right foundation in place for any innovation efforts. Creating the right context is about asking, how do you set the foundation stones up correctly? How do you make sure your soil is fertile before you sow a single seed? How do you structure the organization in a way so that if an idea were to grow, it could potentially turn into an orchard? Even little details of context are important, right down to how do you choose the right furniture, and where to put it within the space.

If you get this step wrong, your organization's existing structures will block the progress of innovation. The ideal way around this in my experience has been, if you're a large organization, especially a publicly listed company, to create a subsidiary that doesn't necessarily impact your publicly reported numbers. Companies will often do this with either corporate venture funds or offshore joint ventures, mainly so they can decrease what's called the earnings-per-share risks of the investment or innovation. If you're a publicly listed company and you start investing in challenger businesses, the analyst community will be very critical of you, because you're basically going outside your mold.

If Coca-Cola all of a sudden began telling us sugary drinks are not the future—that juice or water is—that wouldn't go down well with investors. This would be tantamount to saying that Coca-Cola is dead. In the same vein, if British American Tobacco were to branch out into smoking-cessation products, they would be punished by the analyst community and their own shareholders. Instead, what smart companies in this position do is create a dividing wall between business-as-usual and the upstart innovative subsidiary. It's a structural way to decrease the short-term risk of experimentation, opening up the possibilities for a team to get things approved easily and quickly, particularly in the early stages. You don't want to kill an idea when it's tiny—a little seedling—purely because you're worried about the earnings-per-share risks on a business that's worth less than $50,000.

Another great analogy for this is a botanical garden. Every botanical garden around the world has a separate greenhouse to bring out new species in isolation—away from their regular ecosystem. If you look at botanical gardens here in Singapore, they are famous for orchids and for amazing tropical plants, but for experimental species they work with, they house them in greenhouses until such time they believe they are ready for our ecosystem.

Every client I work with, I insist on spending a solid block of time exploring, and solidifying the 'Innovation Context' before we start on anything else. This point of view is often met with doubt, but in 100% of the time clients thank me as we progress further into the innovation journey.

The Genesis of Wing Money

My innovation career started in 2008, when I was working for ANZ Bank. We were given a challenge that represented a bold departure for the bank's business as usual. Back then, a lot of banks were trying to extend their license abilities in China so they could provide banking services there. One of China's biggest challenges is its very large poor rural population. At the time, there was a big incentive for foreign banks who wanted to get into China to come up with a business model that would allow them to bank in rural China in a cost-effective manner.

At this point, we were seeing early signs of what today we call mobile banking, with the emergence of mobile payments and branches out of Africa, with organizations like South Africa's WIZZIT and Kenya's M-Pesa. These were models that ANZ saw as desirable, so they commissioned an executive named Brad Jones to head up the experimentation phase. From the beginning, Brad and ANZ did something smart: they commercially separated the new entity (now named Wing) from the overall ANZ business, and they achieved this in two key ways.

First, Wing became a wholly-owned subsidiary, with different branding to ANZ's. Even though Wing operated in a country where ANZ was the number one bank, Wing was a separate brand. Second, Wing still relied on ANZ for internal support, but instead of structuring it as an internal agreement, they structured it as a third-party commercial agreement.

This created a culture of independence and innovation from day one: Wing was an independent commercial entity, allowed to fuel its own growth, to explore at its own pace, to hire its own teams, to find its own identity, and to solve its own problems. By setting up those foundations early on, ANZ's oversight was significantly reduced—but in a positive way. With Wing now allowed to go and find its own commercial way in the ecosystem, it was able to challenge the ways of doing business in a way that ANZ never would or could have done.

With this context in place, ANZ was given a solid foundation on which to innovate. We did things with technology that ANZ had never done before. We did things with operations and sales that ANZ had never done before. We went after segments in the market that ANZ had never gone after before. We created a mobile-only bank offering for the rural market in Cambodia. The foundation stones of independence that were put in place for Wing from the start were vital to its success.

Since then, I've been involved in other similar ventures with other organizations. Many of those ventures have presented challenges when the organization didn't get the necessary structural components right first. I've seen at least a dozen instances where companies tried to set up similar banking offerings in other countries—but they did so under an existing brand, and then struggled to get the venture off the ground, simply because the brand enjoy the right level of freedom to explore its own value and composition in the market.

It's the businesses I've worked with that have enjoyed some sort of contextual independence that have also been the most successful. I worked in Bangladesh with Brac Bank, on the creation of a subsidiary called bKash. BKash was granted a simple, independent structural model—a separate entity with the freedom to find its identity and purpose within the commercial ecosystem—and as a result, bKash today is one of the most successful mobile money businesses on the planet. This experience has shown me that providing the right amount of leeway for a new organization to find its purpose, unshackled to the legacy business, can set it up auspiciously in terms of positioning for success.

Whether Startup or Corporation, You Need to Get Context Right

So are startups better positioned for getting context right? Absolutely! Most startups come into the game with no historical legacy, other than the knowledge that their accountants might bring from life or work experience. As a result, they start with a blank canvas to pursue market needs in a way that's totally new.

That's why the most disruptive businesses on the planet are always those that come from the fringes—from a new angle. I'm talking about Airbnb, Uber, and the like. Airbnb could never have emerged from the hotel industry. Structurally, an incumbent just could not have built or maybe even conceptualized the Airbnb model. Uber, too, could never have been spawned by a transport company or car manufacturer. It required a new way of thinking and a blank canvas.

Each of these businesses was the brainchild of a founder who realized there was a problem in the market and decided to tackle the problem in a new way. Each one started with a group of people who were passionate about a particular problem, and they were able to address that in a new way that was ultimately successful. As a result, they have become some of the most disruptive businesses on the planet today.

Moven Bank: A New Way of Banking

A startup I worked with to help build a digital bank in America was a company called Moven (formally known as Moven Bank). Moven was borne out of a frustration shared by myself and my fellow co-founders: we would consult with banks, continually giving them the recipe to build a digital bank, but these banks' own stagnant context meant they would invariably trip over themselves. We were working with a number of established brands, offering them the "genie" for building a digital bank, but they were unable to follow, execute, and let it out of the bottle. What got in the way? Their processes, protocols, and ways of thinking.

We eventually met a couple of venture capitalists who offered to simply give us the money to go build the model we were trying to sell the banks on. With that challenge, we raised capital and started to look at the problem with a clean slate. We tackled the idea of an intelligent conversation between yourself and your money, to build a completely new banking offering called Moven. And today Moven has an extremely powerful spend, save, and live platform that uses behavioral economics to help customers understand how they spend their money.

One of the biggest challenges in the money space is that unless you're an accountant with a spreadsheet, you don't go to the effort of actually understanding how, when, and where you spend your money. Moven was meant to be a way of bringing that feedback into context, where it would be most psychologically helpful—which is basically when you make the purchase. There were two type of purchases that we wanted customers to be connected to. One, what we call subconscious spending—the roughly 5 percent of your disposable income you spend without even thinking. The other one was impulse purchases—that new pair of jeans, or a new bike, a tattoo—that kind of thing.

Our framework connected customers psychologically back with those two areas of spending, based on the hypothesis that doing so would help them improve their cash flow and hence their financial health. We believed that over time, if Moven could make customers more conscious of how they spend money, then we had a better chance at improving how they spent that money. Moven continues today, and it's been extremely successful, with a presence in multiples countries.

If you're a startup, you have a far better chance of actually getting the right context for an innovative company because more than likely you don't carry legacy into that journey. So everything is fresh and a lot of the choices that would foster an innovative company are actually quite logical.

Those decisions will also help how you attract innovative staff, how you build the business, how you bring your offering to market and the likes. The challenge really is for the corporations that say "We already have an incumbent way of doing things; we have a legacy that we carry with us. That legacy is our cash cow today, so we can't change it." So an established company needs to find a way that allows them to keep the cash cow going, but also see the possibilities of a new business opportunity.

Context must be established before you can move on to the next C, culture, in the same way you would build a building. You can't start putting up the walls until you've got a foundation. The one thing that frustrates me the most is seeing amazing talent with the right culture for innovation, but sitting inside an incumbent context, say, within the existing operating model of an insurance company or a bank. Even the most amazing talent, with the most amazing outlook, is going to flounder if the possibilities afforded by its context are limited; they'll hit roadblocks very quickly.

Context is the absolute prerequisite. So what are the elements that make up a success innovation-driving context?

The Elements of Context

Organizations tend to get excited about innovation and go all out on creating an innovative space, with bean bags, Legos, and TV screens—but they often overlook the need to address the entire structure of the organization and thereby create an environment where innovation can flourish, not just a nice room to brainstorm in. Sure, the physical space you operate in is important as well—your normal, partitioned office may not be the most innovative space, so you need to consider how to make a space more innovative. But it shouldn't be the number one thing on your to-do list—remember, some of the most innovative ideas have emerged from basements or garages. Here's a few of the key ingredients you need to get context right.

Strategy

Who's responsible for creating an innovative atmosphere? Business is by its very nature a structured process consisting of routine tasks with systems that need to be followed. As such, innovation must come from the top. It's very much up to the chief executive and the senior leadership team to create an atmosphere in which innovation can flourish. It's their responsibility to create a strategic vision that embraces innovation at its very core. Think about how Google encourages employees to spend 20 percent of their work time on side projects, or Apple's history of asking, "Why does it have to be this way?" The foundational key to success in becoming an innovative company is to create an environment that encourages creative ideas and innovation on a continuous basis. If you're serious about wanting your business to be innovative, you have to establish innovation as a strategic goal. Innovative strategy comes from the top, but it also needs to be ingrained in every part of the organization.

Pay

Innovation and the ability to come up with new products and services customers want is the lifeblood of an organization; it creates profit and enables the organization to survive. Another key consideration is how to pay and incentivize employees to help foster that innovation. The talent that's going to grow innovation for you is unlikely to fall under the same performance management framework you've always had in place. So how do you acknowledge people within the context of their effort and the contributions they make? One of the things most companies get wrong is they try to reward individuals who have innovated within the context of the whole organization, as opposed to making a reward contextual to the effort the employee actually puts in.

There's no one-size-fits-all model here, but since executives normally have pay incentives for increasing revenue, cutting costs, or increasing productivity, why not tie incentive pay to the sales figures for new products? This fosters a broad vision in which executives will consider almost any new idea. It's almost like making people mini-CEOs of a problem set, which is intrinsically rewarding in itself. For instance, if someone is extremely passionate about debt relief, solving world hunger, or making a cycling product—it doesn't matter what it is—they get intrinsic reward from the execution of that vision. That's the reward of the act of innovation.

Further down the chain, at the store or factory level, workers may be less inclined to offer new ideas unless there is a system of recognition and compensation in place. Make it so. Great innovations will generally come from your employees—so make it financially worthwhile for them to share their ideas in house, rather than saving the best ideas for their own potential startups.

Disrupt your Business Model

If an innovative idea were to come about, could you use it to explore an alternative commercial model or create a new, more constructive way of doing your business? Would you be willing to throw your corporate identity into question? Let's say your core business is in pharmaceuticals, but the innovation team's best ideas show the true future isn't so much in pharmaceuticals, but in the treatment of disease. Is this where your future corporate identity lies? Are you willing to revisit the central question of what is the purpose you serve in society? Most organizations focus on solving problems, rather than raising the bar. In the world of innovation, there's high potential that you're going to explore some avenues that challenge your core business model.

Finally, the Innovation Room

Yes, the space matters, if for no other reason than it's a focal point, an area that physically demonstrates the vision of the organization: we are innovative. We encourage innovation, and here is a nice space to be innovative in!

If you don't actually have the physical room for a separate area, think about how you are laying out your office work area. Offering standing desks where people don't have to sit all day, along with a no-assigned-desk policy, can help mix things up a bit. This is entirely possible with laptops and tablets, and it prevents people from getting in a rut. It can also keep individual desks much tidier, which can create a creative environment. Allow workers to bring a pet to work a day or two a week—it could tie up some time, but also create a relaxed environment and help new ideas spring to mind. What about a music room where staff can play or listen to music? The ideas to make an office more creative are as limitless as the ideas you hope to inspire.

Having a more creative space also helps with brainstorming sessions. You can go all out, with the walls covered in writing boards or paper, with feature walls, and inspiring quotes. What you want to focus on the most, though, is creating an inviting space, with some nice comfortable furniture where people can feel creative in. And okay, a bean bag or two can also help!

◦——————◦——————◦

This phase is all about laying the groundwork—making sure the soil is just right for innovation to germinate and grow. This includes putting innovation at the heart of your strategy, recognizing innovation in every part of the company, being open to disrupting your business model, setting apart space and time for innovation, and being open to creating unconventional work spaces, like "hot-desking" with no assigned seating. Once you've set the context for innovation, you then need to enable a culture of innovation within that context, and that's what we'll talk about next.

Chapter 13

CULTURE—HOW INNOVATION
WARS ARE FOUGHT

N ext is the culture that you put within context. How do you build a culture of curiosity? A culture of experimentation, a maker/breaker mentality that will make people want to create (and occasionally destroy) things? How do you decide who to hire? How do you decide to incentivize these people?

In an innovation war, you need to not just sign up the best foot soldiers, platoon leaders, and officers—you also need to train them, to have a structure they can fight well under, and to point them in the right direction. You also need to retain the best. You don't want defectors. You want soldiers to contribute and to move up the ranks. If they have ideas they think will solve something on the field, you want them to be able to speak up, and loudly.

Your employees are in a natural position to understand the nexus of your business operations, product development channels, and customer needs. New growth should naturally be driven from within. Yet often attempts to build a culture of innovation—where employees freely share new ideas, then use fast and cheap processes to get new products or services to market—fall flat.

It's not for lack of effort. I've seen plenty of companies give it their all to build that culture. They put in TV screens and games, and paint the walls inspiring colors. Senior leaders pronounce loudly and widely that innovation is going to be the company's focus. They sometimes even offer cash and prizes to employees who come up with the best ideas. There's a wave of excitement, a flurry of activity … but three months later, it's gone nowhere.

Why? To reiterate: culture should only be tackled after context has been established. The foundation to the building must be there before you start thinking about putting walls up. Culture is about creating an atmosphere that enables individuals and teams to explore the possibilities, the future strategic options of an organization. Culture is an enabler for an innovative company, and is an entire beast in itself.

Culture is the spirit of how a team operates; it's how they interact with each other. What's desirable and what's not desirable? Companies often talk about culture like it's a principle, but it's something more. It's a bit like listing your retail businesses' key selling points as *great service and price.* Customers already expect this. You need to offer more. Typically, organizations tackle the tradition of cultural values in much the same way. Honesty, trust, and other common principles should already be there to make a great organization. It should be taken for granted; therefore, the ones I talk about here are the vital additions.

Curiosity

The first absolutely critical element is curiosity. The best innovators on the planet are children, because they're naturally curious. They'll ask (and re-ask) questions about everything. They'll explore things even though they know they "can't" go there. They have a naturally inquisitive nature that eggs them on to pursue, or to explore, or to adventure in new ways. This curiosity is a foundation stone of culture.

If you're in a highly regulated industry, a lot of people just accept the fact that regulation is the reason they can't do something—even when nobody's had the curiosity to actually go and find out what the actual regulations say. Is the regulation even relevant anymore, or do we need to challenge that regulation?

Most people don't realize that a large portion of the insurance sector's regulations were written in 1983. Times have changed since then, yet very few people are curious to explore further.

Some of the best people to ask questions might not be executives. Maybe it's the staff at the coalface who deal with customers every day. Solicit ideas for innovation from every facet of your business. Don't just rely on the select group employees who are viewed as your "think tank"—ideas can come from anywhere, so make sure everyone feels they can contribute should. Google's a great example of a company that believes every staff member can contribute to innovation. Throw out the organizational chart from time to time and invite everyone to contribute.

Experimentation

A culture of experimentation is one that allows individuals and teams to structure ideas in a way that questions the market. One of the big changes the information age has brought about is the ability to get an answer to almost anything. If you want to know why the sky is blue, you can Google it. If you want to know what the weather is in the next town, you can Google that, too. The answer to almost any question is just a few clicks away. The best innovations in the planet today are based on fact-driven insights. In reality, the whole lean startup movement is based on experimental design to identify facts and test hypotheses—to remove assumptions or guesswork from what you believe is correct and refine our understanding of the actual, underlying reality. This culture of experimentation is how entrepreneurs figure out what the market needs, what problems exist, and how those problems should be solved.

Get experimenting.

Failure

The next one is a culture of failure. This involves realizing, however, that failure is not failure. Failure is a lesson on how not to do something. We might say that 99 percent of all our ideas fail, but what we're actually learning is that 99 out of 100 ways are not the right way of doing something. That's 99 lessons.

The takeaway? Work to eliminate fear of failure among your employees. Fear is an innovation killer, so create an environment where people are free to take risks. This means making sure employees feel safe to propose new, out-there ideas in a way that won't be laughed at, no matter how crazy they sound. There's more than a handful of crazy ideas that have gone on to make millions or change the world as we know it. This also means tolerating failure and viewing it as an innovation lesson.

Adopting this mindset is not easy because most organizations have an internal culture of punishing every single failure, instead of embracing failure as a lesson. That's a very tough mindset to change—for an organization to say, "Look, you wasted $300,000 dollars on an experiment. But guess what? We like this stuff."

Startups deal with failure very well. They might run an experiment, discard the results, and start another experiment the next day. They're continuously experimenting. Why do established companies deal negatively with failure? Financial loss is one part, but it's also because their risk appetite is diminished. The more you think you know how something operates, the more you believe that there's no other way. So you're quick to shoot down every idea or even risk one percent of failure. It's why, for instance, a risk factor of even half a percent is not acceptable for many corporations.

As a result, they spend millions of dollars researching, evaluating, building business cases … and not really doing anything. What they don't realize is that they could have spent a tiny percentage of the money they used on research to run a small experiment, and learn ten times as much in a shorter period of time as a result. Using the lean startup method, most founders can do in three days what it would take a corporation six to twelve months—because the corporation will over-engineer the planning side before doing anything, instead of simply jumping in and learning something.

Ask Why

The next part of building an innovative culture is simply asking why. Asking why helps you connect better with the reason for your existence or the reason for solving a problem. One example is the iPod. It wasn't the first mp3 player—there were already mp3 players from a number of other companies on the market—but it was the first to come in with a very different marketing campaign. When Steve Jobs pitched the iPod, it wasn't as an mp3 player with a bunch of specs. He pitched it with the idea that it was "a thousand songs in your pocket."

To the average, non-tech-savvy consumer, that is the reason for liking the iPod over everything else, because you think, "Ah, there's a thousand songs in my pocket. That's awesome. I get that!" That's the *why*—it gives a deeper meaning to what and how you're building things.

Customer Centric

Startups work well by targeting a customer and building solutions that the customer needs. They're so customer centric that they'll work together to co-create products with their market. "Customer centric" has become a buzzword in most corporate environments, but they often still don't realize the importance of the term. They should be redesigning their whole organization to be customer centric—and I mean everything—corporate structures, the way they go about business, where and how they position their business, and the like. Customer centricity is a culture; it is not just a buzzword. It's a mindset.

The rationale behind customer centricity is one word: empathy. Building a culture of empathy, means you have a deep desire to step into the shoes of an individual to understand their perspective, their problems, their needs, and their wants. Without that connection to what's real, it's very hard to build something meaningful to the market.

When I worked with MetLife we focused on developing an internal culture of innovation. I first did some work to help them understand the requirements for innovation, and then helping them understand how to better implement the cornerstones of a culture that would facilitate innovation. We carried out a cultural educational program based on helping them understand how they could put culture into practice, so that employees across MetLife could start to develop empathy to the market's needs. This is the opposite of the traditional approach of assuming everyone wants insurance—instead, I wanted them to realize there's a more meaningful and impactful way to actually sell and buy insurance. It might be that customers are worried about death, or about getting sick; therefore, understanding the emotional side of that need better positions the organization to build products to meet those needs.

MetLife saw the most success with this approach in Japan, where employees got a firsthand chance to practice methodologies of developing empathy and customer centricity. The training involved setting up a part educational, part practical program within the company. First, we equipped them with the tools and mindset for tackling empathy, then gave them practical exercises to go out and perform.

In this particular case, the MetLife employees came up with some of their own ideas and were encouraged to go out on the streets and run their own experiments—to do a minimum of 100 interviews each to get real feedback and develop real empathy for their ideas—to figure out if those ideas were right or wrong and determine the customer's actual need.

Beyond the Buzzword: Becoming "Agile"

Large, well-established companies have difficulty embracing a culture of innovation, and they also struggle to implement the necessary practices, such as asking why, accepting failure, experimenting, and becoming customer centric. It's difficult partly because of their success. But is it inevitable that they encounter these barriers? No, of course not. The key with culture in an established organization is that if you are able to get context right, then to structure a team in isolation away from the incumbent ways of doing things, the culture of this team, can become a catalyst for the rest of the organization. Only leading by example will they be able to influence the rest of the organization.

This exemplar team is often referred to as an "agile" team. The term "agile" in the business space initially referred to a set of principles and best practices created by software programming teams that had at their heart two major goals: to accelerate work, and to reliably, consistently produce work of high quality. By reducing the burdens of bureaucratic and cumbersome project management, this agile philosophy also freed programmers to work more effectively and efficiently. These agile methodologies have transformed the software industry over the past 25 to 30 years.

The fundamental principles of agile are simple. To attack a problem or project, an organization forms and authorizes a small, motivated, cross-functional, self-managing team. The team's manager typically is from a business function and splits their time between the agile team and key stakeholders. The agile team is then free from distractions and able to get down to work. They will separate top-priority tasks into small modules, and work out how best to get it done, then start building working versions in short cycles known as sprints. The process is open and transparent to all. Members of the agile team might hold very short, often stand-up meetings to review progress and identify potential problems. Any problems or disagreements are solved through experimental feedback loops rather than endless debates or requests to authority. The team tests small working increments with groups of potential customers—in the case of an app, it might be the key features in prototype. If customers get excited, the app (or whatever it is) may be released immediately, even if the powers that be might not fully approve or think it needs more testing. The team will then brainstorm how to improve future cycles and prepare to attack the next priority. This approach solves many problems associated with projects. It reduces interference from above, it involves customers directly early on, it removes impediments, and it increases cross-functional collaboration. It also reduces repetitive, unnecessary meetings and speeds up the whole process.

When we're talking about agile or agility in the innovation space, we're talking about a system that helps create an environment to facilitate design breakthrough solutions to customer problems and develop those solutions economically, often without plotting a course in detail ahead of time or developing comprehensive documentation and specifications. An agile team can get started right away, and if it makes a wrong turn, it's simple enough to make a course correction. What agile does is allow rapid adaptation to the direction and pace of market changes.

One of the most important terms that's come out in the last couple of years is called "the Bimodal IT Model" and although it's been primarily referenced in the IT sphere, it illustrates perfectly how an innovation function can be run in duality with existing business. One group is handed the keep-the-lights-on tasks, the everyday business, the second group works on business-advancing tasks. As Gartner describes it, the first team is traditional, focused on scalability, efficiency, safety and accuracy. The second team focuses on agility, speed, and exploration. Essentially, both are given the possibility of tackling the same problems, but with a new operating model. It also means that the new agile business will have a chance to write new norms. They can find new identity, they can find a new culture, and they can find a new purpose.

<hr />

Culture is all about the *how* of innovation: the principles with which you infuse your workplace to catalyze innovation: focusing on the customer, asking why, experimenting and being willing to fail, being agile in your processes. These are the practices that will open you up to disruption and be better able to recognize and direct innovation as it unfolds within your organization.

More recently, my team has had huge success working with heads of Learning and Development, Human Resources or Innovation taking and learning and development approach to culture transformation. Working with HR a a partner, we can deploy consistent vernacular to ensure that language of an innovative culture finds clarity, consistency and common terminology. It also helps that most companies know how to mobilise budgets when it comes to training and development.

Chapter 14

CAPABILITY—HOW INNOVATION
WARS ARE MANAGED

A n organization requires a series of tools to use so it can be more innovative, and particularly a common operating model with which it can execute ideas. I always say culture is like ploughing a field; **capability** is putting the right seeds in the ground. By using the right frameworks, the right tools to enable that culture, an innovation team can start to turn ideas into reality and foster potential breakthroughs.

So what exactly is capability in an innovation context? Capability is the tools, the methods, and the frameworks the workforce uses within a culture of innovation to make things happen. Design thinking, ideation, agile, the Lean Enterprise model—all those methods come together to keep everyone heading in the same direction, because in a creative space it's easy for everyone to go off on their own creative tangent.

Let's look at some of those tools/capabilities and ways in which I've applied them in the past. You may find these useful in your own innovation efforts.

Persona Modeling

Persona modeling is a concept from the design thinking world that allows an innovator or entrepreneur to document potential market opportunities before designing an experiment and testing the validity of their idea. Let's say you want to build a mobile app for weight loss. You'd begin by looking at a market segment and its goals and pain points to identify how you might target that segment and solve its problems.

The Persona Model is a two-by-two grid. At the top left is *facts*—what do you already know about this segment? At the bottom right is *goals*—what is the potential customer trying to achieve? At the bottom left is *behaviors*—what behaviors are they already exhibiting in pursuit of that goal? Top right is *pains*—what pains, barriers, or obstacles are they encountering in the pursuit of that goal?

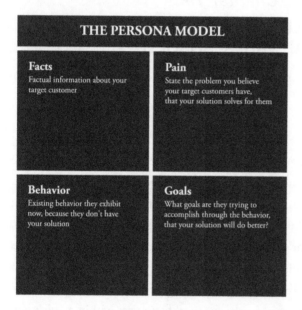

THE PERSONA MODEL

Facts
Factual information about your target customer

Pain
State the problem you believe your target customers have, that your solution solves for them

Behavior
Existing behavior they exhibit now, because they don't have your solution

Goals
What goals are they trying to accomplish through the behavior, that your solution will do better?

Using the weight-loss example, we might look for *Americans* living in *Mississippi* (this is the "fact") who are overweight (the "pain") and want to lose weight (the "goal"). First, to learn enough for us to build a proposition, we need to understand these people's "behaviors." What behaviors is this segment already demonstrating in the pursuit of that goal? That might be counting calories, going to Weight Watchers, signing up for a gym—that kind of thing. Then we would ask what kind of barriers they are currently encountering in the pursuit of their goal. This could be a number of factors: education, affordability, motivation, simplicity, or lack of convenience.

With those boxes completed, we can create the *Three Foundational Hypothesis* for our business venture. The first question of this venture is "Who is the customer?" We can use some demographics to describe them, but we mainly use their behavior to target them. The next question is "What is the problem they're having?" The problem is related to their inability to achieve a goal, so in a way, we can say that *the goal plus the pain is the problem.* Lastly we ask, "What can we do to help them solve that problem?"

The great thing about this model is it allows us to mature our understanding before we write a single line of code. The *existing behaviors plus the goal minus the pain* is what we build—whether it's an app or a technology or a magic pill. It allows us to get a deep empathy for a tested and validated market segment based on behavior to identify early adopters in the market.

Identify Early Adopters

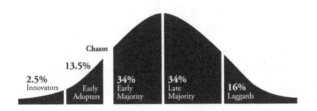

TECHNOLOGY ADOPTION LIFE CYCLE

Early adopters are very important in terms of pushing over the tipping point of adoption in the industry. By identifying the early adopter segment (usually about 13 percent of a market) we've captured not only the first people to use a given product, but people who are actively trying to solve their problem and will help contribute to building a better solution.

Start With Ten, Then a Thousand...

Often entrepreneurs look to the market maturity too early in the market research process and get distracted by generalized market observations that give them no focus. I look at it like this: if you want to serve a million customers, first you have to serve a thousand, and to serve a thousand, first you have to serve ten. With that ten or a thousand, you have targeted focus in your business venture, instead of the distraction of a mass market. The big difference between early adopters and the mass market is early adopters are constantly aware they have a problem and are actively trying to solve that problem, which makes them far easier to sell to and get them to try your product at least once.

I'm not saying all early adopters are going to stick around, because that depends on how well you solve their problem and how well you re-engage them—but they are the most willing participants. Convincing somebody who doesn't think they are obese that they are obese and need to lose weight is extremely hard. It's the same in any other mainstream market. Convincing people that they have a problem worth solving is extremely difficult, so you're better off focusing on people who are already aware that they have a problem.

Once we have that base level assumption we then use that hypothesis to borrow from the Customer Development Model, a framework developed by entrepreneur and business school professor Steve Blank. This model involves going out and testing your core assumptions with the help of your assumed customer and the problem you're going to solve for them. Initially, the biggest and easiest test to do involves asking, "Does this market segment have this problem?" because if they don't have a problem, there's nothing to sell. You'll literally go out on the street to conduct customer interviews and see if you can identify, through, behavior a known market segment that has an active involvement in solving its own problem.

There are different ways to test this, but in the early phases I encourage people to do it "hands-on, face-to-face" for the main reason that, until you have a deep empathy for your market segment, it's very hard to move across the different channels for targeting.

Customer Development Model

CUSTOMER DEVELOPMENT MODEL

Through targeted customer development, you can test one variable at a time in your assumption model. That one variable might be the absence or presence of the problem, the severity of the problem, or the degree of active involvement in solving the problem. But each time, through a series of open-ended questions, you are able to get two things: quantitative data on the pattern of this problem in that customer group, and qualitative data that will help you refine your assumption as you go forward. So, when you go out on the street, you are attempting to identify success criteria by measuring the validity and magnitude of an unknown assumption.

Let's say, for instance, we're looking at a target segment of obese women in their thirties. If 20 percent of obese women in their thirties are actively trying without success to lose weight, we then have reason to believe we are on to a good pattern. You determine what is relevant in terms of success criteria; if you decide 20 percent is your cutoff, and you go and speak to 100 women in their thirties who are obese and less than 20 percent are actively trying to lose weight, then your assumption is invalid. But if greater than 20 percent are actively trying to lose weight, you know you're heading in the right direction. With each cycle in this way, you experiment on one assumption at a time. You pick that assumption based on what you perceive to be the riskiest assumption. For instance, the absence or presence of the customer segment being aware of having that problem is a huge risk, because if this customer segment doesn't know there is a problem, there is nothing to solve for. So you start there. Then your next bottom line might focus more on the actual severity of the problem.

You work systematically through various assumptions, and as you refine your hypothesis, you get closer and closer to the truth on your customer problem/solution hypothesis. The idea isn't to validate your business model, but to invalidate and exclude erroneous assumptions you may hold. This can, of course, take time. For some businesses, this could take a hundred iterations of the customer development cycle. Others might be able to get there more quickly, but with each cycle you want to get closer and closer to a predictable model of finding your customer. Once you're at a point where you can repeatedly identify your customer and they are actively helping to contribute to how you solve their problem, you can then begin to iteratively test and refine solutions to address that problem until you have something that works extremely well.

Even before you write an app or build a product, you can test not only the market's sensitivity, but also how much they're prepared to pay for having their problem solved. Now, paying could include just giving you their email address. That's a form of currency, and it has value because building an email list can be invaluable later, particularly in markets where the customer and the user are not necessarily the same person. For instance, with Google, I might use Google search as a user, but I am not the customer. The customer is an advertiser paying Google for the rankings.

There are three different types of experiments to run: **discovery**, **pitch,** and then **concierge**.

Discovery

The first, as we've discussed, is customer development or discovery, and is very much an exploratory customer interview and/or survey approach.

Pitch Testing

The next is pitch testing. Once you can repeatedly identify a customer with a problem, what you're saying is, "I can solve your problem. Would you like me to do so, in exchange for something of value?" That could be a dollar; it could also be an email address or a telephone number. What you're really testing is the customer's willingness to give you something of value in exchange for the promise of solving their problem.

Over time, the accumulation of 'value' demonstrate the idea is growing in potential, but you now have an objective, pre-revenue way to measure that value.

Concierge Testing

Once you are able to identify the segment that's willing to pay for it, you should consider pretending to solve their problem for the pure purpose of getting feedback on how you delivered the experience. This is the third kind of testing.

I'll give you an example. When I was in the United States mentoring a bunch of startups I encountered one called Last Minute Haircuts. They wanted to be, for the lack of a better word, the HotelQuickly of last-minute hair care—based on the app that allows users to find discounted hotels around the world. They felt that this was a huge market with huge potential, because so many salons often go under-utilized and could potentially fulfil demand to anyone in close proximity.

So, they got out on the street and started approaching their first target segment, busy professional women. What they found very quickly through this customer development was that women don't do last-minute haircuts. They plan their next haircut four, five, or six weeks in advance. In fact, the vast majority of women book their next haircut when they are leaving their current one. So, the Last Minute Haircuts team figured out that their target segment had to change. They had encountered some soft data when speaking to one woman whose boyfriend had said, "Actually, I need a haircut." And so, they realized that a man was more likely to want a last-minute haircut because guys are less likely to plan their haircuts.

Last Minute Haircuts then pivoted their proposition to busy professional males. They had a team of six men and women who were doing customer development, and they were able, with a high degree of conversion, to get men to adopt their offering. What they were doing was concierge testing—where they eventually got very good at targeting men based on characteristics, behavior, and clothing, and were able to convert a high percentage of these men. They quickly found they were making a healthy margin—$4 or $5 per haircut—referring them to local hairdressers, and were able to "sell" around 500 haircuts a day—before they even considered building their app.

When they finally did build the app, Last Minute Haircuts knew their customer so well that they knew it would be a success.

Prototyping

Next, let's enter the world of prototyping, where you build something—whether it's physical, an app, or something else—but you build only enough to test the market response to it. You don't build all 100 features on day one. You build the ones that are vital to the proposition and test the response to them. You start by bringing in potential customers, either through content marketing, social media, or advertising. Then you test which channels and messages are going to attract and convert people. You can build up a mailing list, and even allow people to pre-order products. What you're essentially trying to do is sell the product to the market in an experimental manner to pre-validate demand.

Once the context and the culture underneath it exists, capability can flourish in the innovation team. One of the challenges in the innovation world is to beat the unknown factor. Decisions will often be won by the loudest person in the room, or the person who seems to be the most informed—but by using models, we take the speculation out of the process and rely instead on hard data—on facts. When you make a decision about the color of a button, or the type of customer that you're after, you want hard data to back that decision.

Don't get me wrong: innovation and entrepreneurship is an art, but it's also a science too!

Capability is where the rubber really meets the road. It's where you take your innovation war to the streets, testing and retesting your assumptions, leaving no stone unturned and no sacred cow unscrutinized. It's in this layer that you come more fully into your true capability for standalone innovation—but as we'll learn in the next chapter, what differentiates world-class innovators from the rest of the pack is their ability to combine forces.

Chapter 15

COLLABORATION—HOW
INNOVATION WARS ARE WON

T he 4th C is *collaboration*. How do you go beyond your own capability? How do you work with organizations you've never worked with before? Charles Darwin said it well: "In the long history of humankind (and animal kind, too) those who learned to collaborate and improvise most effectively have prevailed." Innovation, collaboration, and improvisation are necessary forces in shaping nature, but they've also become vitally important for business organizations, and for society.

The 4C framework was originally just 3Cs—Context, Culture, and Capability, but I found that with only those 3Cs, I was continually hitting roadblocks with clients. That's where collaboration came in. Collaboration is all about how well an organization understands its core capabilities and can plug them into a larger value chain.

You're Gonna Need Someone On Your Side

If a country's involved in a war, history shows it generally doesn't happen alone. You're going to need someone on your side. It doesn't even have to be on a massive scale, as in World War II, in which practically all the countries of the world picked sides, dividing themselves between the Allies and the Axis. Smaller conflicts have all seen collaboration. South Korea had the Americans, North Korea had the Chinese—initially in smaller training and advisory roles—that eventually spilled over into full military support. Most countries involved in a conflict receive some help. Few go it totally alone.

It's practically the same with an Innovation War. Few companies are experts at everything. The best of the best actually do just a few things, but do them very well. This also means they don't have the depth of experience in other (often complementary) industries to reach out and create something truly innovative and new to their industry. They need to partner.

Often when we think of great innovations that have come into being, we think of them as the invention from a sudden brainstorm of one individual—a "light bulb moment," or the apple falling on Isaac Newton's head. While there may indeed be some great examples of these kinds of innovative moments, many companies are finding that innovation is often produced iteratively, over time, by a collective of people working within different organizations.

Collaboration is the result of the realization that you can't do everything yourself. You don't have all the answers, and you will never have all the skills required to do something—and in fact sometimes working with other organizations will indeed produce breakthroughs that you wouldn't achieve by working within. You are not a god—even though this is a complex many innovators have.

Effective collaboration requires that you look for complementary capabilities, in which one plus one equals eleven. *The whole is greater than the sum of its parts.* As an example, most vineyards don't bottle their own wine; they get a professional bottler to do it, and a distribution company to deliver it. Together they are stronger.

As another example, think of the mortgage sector. Say you're a bank. One of your largest and most profitable products is your mortgage business. But when a customer buys a mortgage from you—that's not the whole process—the whole process is buying a *home*. The journey and value chain in buying a home is significantly larger than just the application of credit. What this means for a bank is that there are players upstream and downstream that can add value to the bank's business. So how does the bank that wants to help you buy a home consider potential collaborations, or even building new capabilities within that broader value chain? Sometimes they'll do it themselves, or sometimes they'll do it with a logical partner—by joining forces with a moving company, for example.

There's no one-size-fits-all approach, but understanding your capabilities allows you to be open about what you're good at and what you're not, and helps you understand who you could do with on your side.

Think Outside the Box—And if You Can't, Find Someone Who Can

One of the things I constantly encourage large corporations that do not have the capacity to think outside of the box to do is to partner up with startups and small entrepreneurs that do think beyond their own box and attempt to create something truly innovative. This is a simple way for an organization to look at their challenges and opportunities in a very different way: get an outsider involved. Of course, an organization needs to collaborate effectively internally as well, but almost every organization will benefit from the input of an outsider.

Collaboration also adds value and saves time. For instance, with my business consulting I work with virtual systems in the Philippines. I work with outsourcing companies. I work with cloud labor firms in Singapore. I work with other partners in my supply chain. All of these collaborations help me leverage the time I have so I can focus on higher-value work. Technology firms tend to do collaboration very well. Silicon Valley is a collaborative ecosystem unto itself. The enduring relationship between Intel and Microsoft is an obvious example, but Cisco Systems frequently collaborates with both firms. There are hundreds of other long-standing examples.

Technology Shifts Assist Collaboration

Many of what we might call "technology shifts" have also come out of collaboration. Take Amazon—they had a bunch of merchants selling on the Amazon.com site, companies and individuals that did not have their own web hosting or application hosting capabilities. What Amazon realized is that they were very good at managing web services, so they started offering it to their merchants. With that, Amazon Web Services (AWS) was born. AWS makes infrastructure management easier and more scalable en masse. As a result, today a huge number of startups realize that it's wasteful and time-consuming to run their own infrastructure—and why bother when they can just pay based on a variable cost model to a collaborator like AWS?

Technology has also flattened the marketplace, making it a much more level playing field and opening up collaboration across geographical borders. Technology has also reduced barriers to market entry around the world. You can get online in Berlin and offer your web design services to a company in Beijing. Technology shifts allows buyers and sellers to connect and do business from anywhere in the world.

Technology shifts also mean that the world is getting smaller. Until as recently as five or so years ago, businesses tended to hire people who lived close to their offices, or at least in the same geographical area. Remote working or working from home wasn't on the table, and outsourcing to foreign countries was pretty much unheard of. Today, for a growing number of companies, allowing employees to do at least some of their work from home has become totally acceptable. Virtual workers are able to collaborate with people based in an office, and work can be completed from anywhere in the world as long as you have access to a power port to charge your tablet and phone and a decent WiFi signal.

Wing Money

I was in Cambodia in 2008 when we were busy building Wing Money. We realized that our capability was largely on the back-end payments side. We had very little expertise in market distribution, very little expertise operating outside the urban areas, and very little expertise in operating a low-value, high-volume business. As a result, we decided to partner with the six major telcos in the country to help with the distribution of the product, particularly in the rural markets of Cambodia. In that way, we did not have to build a parallel logistics system, a parallel sales system, or a parallel customer service system. The telco partners became a logical and value-added extension of our capability.

We also partnered with collaborators in the microfinance space that were doing a lot of high-volume, low-value merchant transactions with the rural population. With our capability plus their ecosystem, all of a sudden Wing became the very first electronic microfinance payments platform in the world. We did not want to encroach on the business of the microfinance institution, and they had no intention of entering the payments business. But together, we were able to create something innovative outside both of our core areas of business focus. Once again, one plus one was equal to eleven.

Innovation at the Intersection of Industries

If you look at where disruption is going to come from, particularly in the next decade, it's not going to come within the industries as they are known today— it's going to come from the *intersection* of industries. Big data, cloud, social networking, and mobility have driven digital disruption across many industries. You could say we are in the midst of an unparalleled storm of innovation.

As we talked about in Chapter 5, retail, insurance, banking, and education are just a few of the industries ripe for disruption. There's also a lot of potential for innovation at the intersection of those industries, for two reasons. One, the incumbents in those industries are often too blind to innovate on the fringes of their own system, or engage in value-chain based innovations, where two industries together become stronger than one. The best example I can give is of healthcare technology today and insurance today—they don't collaborate very well. But it is in the insurance company's commercial interests to assist you to live a longer and a healthier life. So why would they not partner in the healthcare sector and do more in the preventive space to ensure that you are healthier and live longer, thus boosting the profitability of the insurance *and* the health insurance businesses? The only way they can do that is to work with someone in the preventive health space.

The intersection of industries allows diverse ideas from different people in dissimilar industries with vastly different cultures to collide and create innovation. Collaboration is vital. Dissimilar groups come up with far more ideas than homogenous groups. Having a transparent meeting of minds at the intersection of industries enables outsiders to open up with left-field ideas about your industry—ones you'd never have thought of—and you may be able to offer the same kinds of new insights into their industry, as well. This is the space in which interesting conversations can happen and from which incredibly new innovative ideas can spring.

Looking more closely at the 4Cs, you'll start to realize that they are not mutually exclusive; rather, they are a series of complementary building blocks. They allow a company to go from where they are today toward being more innovative, and there is a deliberate order of operations. You must start with context—you must get the foundations right. You must then move to culture to fertilize the soil in order to get people prepared to do things the right way. When you move to capability it's actually about execution—and capability and collaboration always overlap.

In fact, the 4Cs also represent a cycle of how you act to become an innovative company and stay innovative. Over time you can go back and revisit how you set your context, or how you developed your culture, but you must know and start with the foundations, so you can put your first foot in the right direction.

The smartest innovators know their limits. They understand and acknowledge the depth of capabilities that their organization can never hope to possess. They combine this awareness with a recognition of the capabilities that exist in organizations outside their company, as well as how to engage those organizations to create a win-win for all sides. When collaboration becomes a priority measure, the world opens up for the would-be innovator.

PART 4

LOOKING INWARD: WHAT IT TAKES TO BE A FUTURE INNOVATOR

Chapter 16

THE DNA OF TOMORROW'S INNOVATION SOLDIER

D o a study. Ask a group of kindergarten kids: "Do you think you're creative?" You can be sure about 95 percent of them will answer "Yes." Try again with fifth graders, and you'll see the proportion drop to somewhere around half. By the time they're seniors in high school, there will only be a few hands up. As Picasso said, "Every child is born an artist. The problems begin once we start to grow up."

The question then is, how creative, how innovative are these young men and women going to be by the time they hit the business world? Schooling, society, and the general system we have in place tends to knock the creativity out of the great mass of people. Humans are taught from a young age to fit in, to the point where only a few individuals drift through the net with the ability to be truly, naturally, creative and innovative. The ramifications seem dire—yet truly innovative individuals still exist.

Jeff Bezos, founder and CEO of Amazon.com. Larry Page, co-founder and current CEO of Google. Sergey Brin, multi-billionaire co-founder of Google. Elon Musk, co-founder of Paypal and founder of Tesla and Space-X. Reid

Hoffman, founder of LinkedIn. Richard Branson, colorful founder of Virgin Group. Ray Kurzweil, revolutionary futurist, celebrated inventor, innovative researcher, and bestselling author. Dean Kamen, inventor of the pioneering Segway. Marc Benioff, founder of software company Salesforce. Tim Brown, CEO and president of IDEO, a pioneering international design firm. Martine Rothblatt, founder of United Therapeutics, a medical biotech company. Larry Ellison, co-founder and CEO of Oracle. Michael Dell, founder and CEO of Dell Computers. Hiroshi Mikitani, co-founder and CEO of Rakuten, Japan's largest e-commerce company. Jony Ive, world-renowned product designer. Robert De Pera, founder of Ubiquiti Networks, a pioneering wireless technology company. Marissa Mayer, former CEO of Yahoo. Shai Agassi, Israeli entrepreneur and founder of the unsuccessful but innovative company Better Place, which pioneered a unique battery technology for electric cars. Salman Khan, founder of Khan Academy, a free, nonprofit online education platform. To name a few.

Are these innovators born, or can you create one? Can a person make themselves more innovative? Both are intriguing questions. You can train an ordinary soldier. The US Marines can take a candidate off the street and through training, discipline, and education make a soldier out of him or her. Creating an innovation soldier (while not impossible) is a little trickier. Based on my own experience, I lean toward the idea that innovators are both born with a certain genetic predisposition, and are made through active effort, struggle, and learning. I would agree that many individuals are naturally born more creative. Just as John Lennon may have been born with certain skills that allowed him to create innovations within the music world, so too was Steve Jobs born with a certain innovative DNA that made him more likely to succeed in business. In fact, major research projects carried out on the creative abilities of identical and fraternal twins tend to back this up, with findings showing 25–40 percent of what we do innovatively stems from genetics, while 60–75 percent of our innovation skills come from learning. So nurture does trump nature as far as creativity goes.

It's great to have an innovative organization, but without innovative people, that organization is going to struggle to achieve its innovative objectives, to create transformation and see its ideas come to fruition. Innovators provide the lifeblood to an organization, helping to ensure change and growth. And many organizations are realizing they can't keep doing the *same old, same old* forever. This is perhaps the reason for the trend in the past ten years to put visionary entrepreneurs like Apple's Steve Jobs, eBay's Pierre Omidyar, Amazon's Jeff Bezos, and P&G's A.G. Lafley on a pedestal. Just how do these people come up with such groundbreaking ideas time after time? Is there some way we can dissect the inner workings of these grand masters' minds, or analyze their DNA, perhaps? What would it tell us about the methods in which innovation happens?

An organization that seeks innovation does need to be a little more selective than the US Army. You need to find those individuals with innovation DNA—in fact, they may already be in your company and you just don't know it yet—and activate them. You need to nurture them, and provide an environment that will help them grow. When we talk about the DNA of tomorrow's innovation soldier, we're actually referring to three key questions business leaders need to ask themselves if they want to get serious about innovation at the individual level:

1. How can I find innovative employees?
2. How can I create innovative employees?
3. How can I myself become more innovative?

"Innovation," Steve Jobs said, "comes from people meeting up in the hallways or calling each other at 10:30 at night with a new idea, or because they realized something that shoots holes in how we've been thinking about a problem. It's ad hoc meetings of six people called by someone who thinks he has figured out the coolest new thing ever and who wants to know what other people think of his idea."

The 4P framework is the other half of my recipe for innovation. I came up with the 4Ps to understand what separates truly innovative individuals from the people who are also trying to innovate but are not yet succeeding. Because it takes more than just a nice, creative environment for innovation to flourish. It takes having the right people who also have the right stuff—the right DNA.

Just as the 4Cs we discussed previously can create an organization more adaptive to change and more conducive to innovative practices, the 4Ps are four principles that offer the same lessons to an individual, serving as a guide over and above one's job description or function inside the organization. These principles are meant to guide each person on their individual innovation path no matter what is thrown at them. They are:

- Problem
- Passion
- Purpose
- Principles

Innovative individuals are driven by solving problems that they are passionate about. They find purpose and self-worth through that pursuit and leverage their experience and principles to guide them. They have diverse networks and constantly seek advice. They think beyond the obvious and aren't afraid to try new things. In the next four chapters, we'll discuss how to identify them and cultivate them within your organization.

Chapter 17

PROBLEM—THE INDIVIDUAL'S INTERNAL WAR TO MAKE A DIFFERENCE

A deep connection with the problem you're trying to solve is a crucial part of driving innovation. A regular soldier follows orders. An innovation soldier follows his or her passion to find a problem that resonates with them—and once they've sunk their teeth into that problem, they are pretty likely, over time, to solve it. We've talked a little bit about the makeup of the innovation soldier, to understand what traits an individual must possess in order to drive innovation. Now we're going to look at the first of the four Ps that make up the DNA of the innovation soldier—*Problem.*

The Problem First, Independent of the Solution

The reason I put so much emphasis on the problem is because people often focus on "how" they're going to solve something rather than the "what" they're actually trying to solve. You hear a lot of people saying, "I want to build an app for this," or, "I want to be the Uber for pizza," or, "I want to be the Airbnb for restaurants." The issue with that kind of thinking is they're already framing the idea that's driving their change, or their innovation, through *how* they solve things as opposed to *what* they're actually solving. This is the hammer in search of a nail. Does pizza really need an "Uber"? Or is there a more pressing pizza problem that requires a different solution?

When I was in Cambodia in 2008, I helped build a financial inclusion product called Wing Money. Our aim with Wing Money was to build an inclusive instrument that would alleviate people at the bottom of the pyramid from something called the property premiere—they paid a premium price for the most basic of services. This was our problem.

In trying to solve that problem, we had free reign to determine how to do so. We could consider as many possibilities as we liked to address the problem. We considered cell phone payments, we considered banking products, we considered cards, and other products that could have solved their need. We were agnostic as to the nature of the solution. We focused on getting deep empathy on the problem before we married ourselves to a certain direction or a resolution. As a result, we ended up building a product that fitted the market problems so well that almost half the country's GDP is being processed through Wing Money.

By connecting with the problem first and being agnostic about the solution, innovators have more range to address a market need. But identifying the problem sometimes means going beyond the face-level evidence. Objective customer empathy doesn't just mean listening to what your customers *say*. You may recall the example of Henry Ford from Chapter 10, who famously said, "If I'd asked my customers what they wanted, they would have just asked for a faster horse." He realized that the horse was just a solution. By focusing on the actual problem, Ford was able to get closer to the nature of the problem, instead of focusing on how he was going to solve it. If he hadn't done that, he would have never built the car. He was thinking at a conceptual level of a mode of transport as opposed to constraining himself on the basis how to improve a horse.

The other thing that makes the problem important is that the road of innovation can be painful, filled with frustration, failure, and resistance. In order to push through those barriers, one needs to have a deep motivation to persevere. The only way to persevere is to not be married to how you're going to solve a problem—to make the problem itself what you're passionate about—because the problem itself will never go away, until you solve it.

Being attached to the *how* is tricky business. Your how for solving a problem could go away, if the market invalidates it, or it becomes illegal, the technology you need is unavailable or unaffordability, or any other number of setbacks. What then?

Innovate or Die: Literally

One of the most effective forms of innovation on the planet is *innovation out of necessity*. You don't tend to see this in developed economies—you see it mostly in emerging markets, where you'll find people in states of poverty, with scarce resources, but who are innovating, because without it they wouldn't survive. Suboptimal conditions are a key catalyst for molding innovative people.

One example is William Kamkwamba, a Malawian innovator, engineer, and author who gained fame in 2002 when he built a windmill to power electrical appliances in his family's house utilizing blue gum trees, bicycle parts, and materials collected in a local scrapyard. His need for a windmill was real. Reading a textbook and watching YouTube videos on a borrowed cell phone allowed him to find the raw materials and develop the skills to build the first windmill in SubSaharan Africa. He had a deep connection to the problem, independent of how it's solved.

Founder—Problem Fit

The best startup founders on the planet have what's called *founder—problem fit*. Founder—problem fit is literally an indicator of a match between the founder and the problem they are going after. What compelled the founder to start the business? What experiences has this founder has in this space? What unique insight does the founder have in order to succeed? Founders that start businesses in spaces where they have little insider knowledge typically struggle. On the other hand, if they do bring real insight, they can identify real opportunities, go fast, and build a great business.

Twitter founder Jack Dorsey was extremely passionate about the patterns of analysis of monitoring the emergency services ecosystem of New York, and his brainchild (originally called Odeo) was born out this fascination with the New York City dispatch system. Twitter as we know it today is still based on the core premise of an emergency system or a dispatch system—short messages, commands passed across an open network, an open fire hose, and specific keywords used to alert the network around questions of urgency, allocation, and important topics.

What about another innovation, the biggest of the past 30 years? The World Wide Web. When Tim Berners-Lee wanted to present his ideas at a conference in San Antonio back in 1991, the conference organizers rejected his paper, and relegated it to the poster session, usually a spot reserved for graduate students and fringe types. Few people who were privy to the embryonic Internet in the early years regarded it as technically great, or even worthwhile invention.

Berners-Lee talked about how web links could resolve addresses to servers located anywhere in the world. He didn't have much time, and made his points in a hurried manner as he struggled to fit it all in. The response was, if anything, subdued, but Berners-Lee wasn't fazed because he had a passion about about solving a problem that he knew the Internet could solve.

Find someone who is deeply passionate about the problem and will own it—whether that's the startup's founder, the head of a department, or a soldier on the ground. A passionate individual has the best chance of making that idea work, because they have a great fit with the problem.

Reframe and Reframe

You'll often find that the most creative people are those who are finding new ways to solve a problem, whether it's an old or a new problem. Businesses such as Instagram, Facebook, and Airbnb are all ways of reframing an old problem in context of new capabilities, new insights, and new information in the modern era. Look at Uber: all Uber did is change the way people look at transportation, in light of a digital economy. The problem is still transport, but how it gets sold becomes different, because it's applied in a different way and a different context. Who in the transport sector would come up with such an innovation in the transport sector? I can guarantee it won't be just be anyone—if you're not passionate about transport you'll never develop the deep understanding of, and affinity for, the problems that could be solved in this area.

As Above, So Below

Apple is an innovative company, and they continue to be innovative. Steve Jobs himself was a great innovator as an individual, and he planted his work firmly in the 4Ps—beginning with identifying the right problem, one he was passionate to solve. Within the problem they find their purpose, they find their own self-worth in solving that problem. He was also always governed by a series of principles—and for Jobs, a key principle was that you can never ask deeply enough—never ask "Why has it always been like that," "why does is it have to be like that?" Jobs was great at identifying problems—because in a sense, for him, the status quo was the problem. There were always things to be solved or made better. This is a large part of what made Steve Jobs a fantastic innovator, and his company so good at what they do.

As in the case of Jobs, does innovation through problem identification always have to come from above? Of course not. Your front line staff, the ones who deal with customers on a daily basis, are also the ones most likely to raise problems or identify opportunities to improve the customer experience. The person on the front lines who raises a problem is often the person who's most passionate about solving it—either because it allows them to serve their direct customer better or it allows them to have more satisfaction in the way they go about their work. You can marry the fertilization of culture, the tool sets of capability, along with the person who wants to work on a particular problem.

The process of identifying the problem-sets your organization needs to tackle comes through the culture and capability frameworks we discussed in Chapters 12 and 13, but once you have identified a problem, it's not a matter of *imposing* the work of solving that problem on people, but rather *finding* the people who are passionate about working on that problem. So how do you find people with the passion to solve a problem? That's what we'll talk about next.

Chapter 18

PASSION—THE UNSTOPPABLE FORCE
OF INNOVATION SOLDIERS

M ost soldiers are passionate. Americans love their country, and it's reflected in the passion of the various armed services. The Viet-Cong probably loved their country too, and were passionate enough to fight to the death to repel invading nations during the Vietnam War. It's hard to defeat someone who is passionate about what he or she is fighting for. It's the same too for our modern day innovation soldier. Of course first of all, you have to find something that you're passionate about, and that can be a cause, a company, a product or an idea. If you think you have an idea that's world-changing, you're going to be passionate about it. That's for sure.

Passion is about intrinsic desire or motivation, separate from material incentives that allows people to reward themselves in the absence of any actual rewards. The best startup founders and innovators on the planet don't do it because they want to sell their company for a billion dollars or because they want to create the sexiest, coolest technology. It's because they possess an intrinsic passion that is fueled by the process of solving a problem.

Granted, passion comes with its opposite and that is for lack of better word, depression, but passion can only be measured because of the existence of this opposing force. It's yin and yang. If I use the analogy of a rollercoaster, what you'll find in the standard corporate environment is that the rollercoaster of typical employment tends to be flatter. But would you want to ride a rollercoaster if the whole thing were flat?

Remember, in order to achieve what only 5 percent of people achieve, you have to do what 95 percent of people will not do. Many people look at a rollercoaster and decide it's beyond their current risk tolerances or fears. They'll see the loops and drops, and the high speeds, and think *Whoa, that's beyond me!* Passionate people desire the extremes that organizations want, because that passion fuels their ability to tolerate the ups and downs of their rollercoaster ride. It's what allows them to do the things that the large majority of others won't.

How do you create those high highs, those soaring peaks? That only comes through the deep passion that drives you to go beyond logic, beyond reason, beyond risk tolerances, and to push you into thinking beyond the current framework. Yes, Star Trek fans, to boldly go where no one has gone before.

In fact, the best entrepreneurs on the planet find serenity in the most extremes of their passion, in much the same way as a world champion Grand Prix motorcycle racer. A champion can push a motorcycle well beyond what anyone else on the planet can do—and they find it therapeutic. They find clarity in doing things that others will not do. The majority of competitive motorcycle riders that attempt to ride Grand Prix might reach 80 or 90 percent of the performance potential of a world champion, but they don't have the passion that brings them into that degree of serenity. They'll never find the same performance clarity possessed by those people at the very top—a clarity that comes only by doing something that you *must* do for your own peace of mind. Remember, the vast majority of entrepreneurs don't get paid for the first year or so they work on an idea. You have to have a passion for the problem, and that passion threshold must be above the reward of anything else.

The Technology Adoption Life Cycle Model

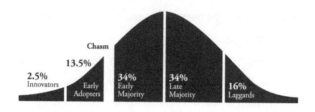

TECHNOLOGY ADOPTION LIFE CYCLE

If we return to Geoffrey Moore's Technology Adoption Life Cycle Model, the innovators are the ones on the far left. These are the people who are not only aware of the existence of a problem, but who actively want to be a part of creating a solution—and they desire to do this so much that they would do it even without getting paid. Everyone tells them they're crazy, or there's no value in it, or they're up against regulator rules, or they're going up against the biggest competitors in the planet—yet they continue to pursue it, even in the face of those adversities. The best examples of people who are the most passionate are the ones who start movements. Dr Martin Luther King, Nelson Mandela, or Harvey Milk—people who have been the advocates of a cause. Commercial passion is different—I do not want to insensitively equate the two realms—but the individuals who lead these causes share similar patterns with entrepreneurs in terms of their behavior and psychology. Mandela endured prison. King and Milk endured death threats and were eventually assassinated. While it's less dramatic in the business world, if you're an innovator, you'll discover that you're often forced to swim upstream. Endurance is key. Only the most passionate will be able to dig deep enough to find a continuous source of energy beyond traditional reward schemes.

Identify People with Passion

So how do you identify people to whom the intrinsic reward for something they're working on is not contingent on the material reward? In truth, it's very hard to design for the identification of these people. These people are often self-selecting. They'll often be externally visible and already demonstrating a number of the traits that we talked about in culture. They demonstrate curiosity, open experimentation, resilience. In an organization, the people who are often the most identifiable are those that are the most outspoken. The important thing once you've identified these individuals is to figure out *what* they're passionate about. Sometimes you'll find what they're passionate about is the structure of the organization.

Companies should also keep in mind the role of context in instilling passion in employees. One of the biggest challenges when it comes to finding passionate innovators is that often the passion may not even be apparent. It will take the right context to awaken that passion. Often a person will take on a role as they think it's a nice one for their career, but eventually develop as a strong connection with it—this is a common occurrence.

People can suddenly become more passionate about their job, because they're working in a context that fuels their passion. I often see this when people make a shift to working from home, or in a new country, and suddenly find the passion to tackle a problem or issue. For these employees, the typical attendance requirements don't always work, and that's just one thing for a company to consider in setting the right context for some employees to latch onto an innovation mindset. Are you beginning to see how the 4Cs and the 4Ps all work in tandem? It's a matter of getting all of them aligned.

An executive I worked with at Wing Money, Brad Jones, had previously enjoyed an established banking career. But the moment he connected with the problem of financial inclusion, he changed gears in his life. All of a sudden, he was emboldened to challenge his stakeholders. He was prepared to tell them when they were wrong, and even when the organization faced separation from ANZ, he connected himself more passionately with the mission of the problem set of Wing Money than with the strategic direction of the corporation above it. He was a man on a mission. As a result, he's now made a career out of solving the problem of technology-driven financial inclusion. Without ANZ even knowing it, he was one of the best people for that job, purely because he connected so strongly with the problem they were trying to fix, as opposed to how they were trying to fix it.

What concrete ways can potentially passionate employees be unearthed in an interview process? There are definitely questions you can ask. The challenge lies in the fact that those questions often pertain to an individual's personal life as opposed to their professional life. This is why it's important for companies to ask questions about what a potential employee likes to do in their life outside the office. What are their hobbies? Where do they travel? What languages have they studied?

Companies spend time writing jobs descriptions and posting jobs, hoping they can impose those roles on people—rather than figuring out who's passionate about solving a problem, independent of *how* they might do it. These companies have to realize the *how* may not necessarily be known to anyone. The job might consist entirely in *finding* the how.

Takeaways

- For individuals, look for things you're passionate about, ones you'd do even if you weren't being rewarded financially.
- For organizations, if you have a task, it's to find employees who are passionate about a problem. They may already be in your organization. They may not even know solving that problem is their passion.

True innovation soldiers are those who are willing, able, and determined to break paradigms. They have a passion about the problem in front of them that can't be defined or defied. They're the people who find meaning and excitement beyond the bounds of how others measure success, gauge risk, or embrace fear. The next P is purpose, and it's an organic extension of passion.

Chapter 19

PURPOSE—HOW INNOVATION SOLDIERS DEVELOP THEIR SKILLS AND INSTINCTS

B efore we talk about purpose, let's recap Maslow's Hierarchy of Needs for anyone who's a bit rusty. The Hierarchy of Needs is a well-known theory in psychology proposed by Abraham Maslow in his 1943 paper "A Theory of Human Motivation."

After much thought, Maslow concluded that we search for things that will fulfill our needs for survival first, and then our emotional happiness and self-fulfillment later. Physiological needs are these things that we *must* have to exist—things like food, water, warmth, shelter, and rest. Without

MASLOW'S HIERARCHY OF NEEDS

SELF-ACTUALIZATION: achieving one's full potential, including creative activities — Self-fulfillment needs

ESTEEM NEEDS: prestige and feeling of accomplishment

BELONGINGNESS AND LOVE NEEDS: intimate relationships, friends — Psychological needs

SAFETY NEEDS: security, safety — Basic needs

PHYSIOLOGICAL NEEDS: food, water, warmth, rest

these basic needs met, we'd die; without needs further up the pyramid, we may well still survive—just not as happily as we could.

Next in Maslow's model are our safety needs: these are the things we need to feel protected against external influences, from both man and nature. In a modern context this level may include having a steady, well-paying job; owning a home; being able to afford good healthcare; and living in a safe neighborhood.

At the midway point, the needs start to become psychological; perhaps less life-threatening, but still important to our overall well-being and happiness. People desire social connection, the desire to feel loved and belonging.

The penultimate layer of the hierarchy describes the importance of self-esteem, which depends upon the light in which we perceive ourselves: positive or negative. Do we feel fully recognized for what we have done and achieved?

The top of the pyramid and final stage of Maslow's Hierarchy of Needs is self-actualization. Fulfilling the requirements of this stage allows us to feel as though we've reached our potential and achieved something worthy of recognition in our lives. At this point, we will be able to see through what others say; we will be content with ourselves and our own lives, and other people's opinions will become far less important or soul-destroying.

So where does purpose fit into all of this? Purpose could be said to sit somewhere between self-esteem and self-actualization on Maslow's diagram. Purpose is doing something more deeply fulfilling than anything else, it's something that makes great employees, great innovators, great entrepreneurs, and great humanitarians. Finding your purpose is finding your calling; it could be solving a problem, it could be creating something fantastically innovative and new, or it could be something else out of left field, but whatever it is—it allows you to do something that most entrepreneurs and innovators struggle with—and that's focus. Overall innovators and entrepreneurs are fantastic in terms of connecting dots and seeing patterns in society, but it's also a weakness for them because it allows them to get distracted very easily. With purpose they will work till 3 AM because they want to do it, because they feel it's a mission in life to alleviate poverty, or to create the next mobile technology or social network. If you look at the story of Mark

Zuckerberg in the creation of Facebook, he found his own purpose in creating this the digital social construct, he loved doing that and solving the broader problem in society.

One of the great things about people finding purpose is that they may not have the necessary skills to pursue that purpose from the start. But what they do is find the weapons to make that possible—an entrepreneur might go learn some code so they can build a prototype to solve the problem that's nagging at them. They'll look high and low for the sources of funding they need to get their idea off the ground. They'll push through seemingly insurmountable barriers, one that would hold most people back.

In the corporate world, people often think, "Okay, my job is to be a business analyst/manager/customer service rep, so I won't go beyond that." But for true innovation soldiers, there are no barriers—they will step outside the boxes imposed on them and find the resources required to achieve their purpose. In doing so, they also find great happiness—genuine, visible enthusiasm for what they are doing. This is visible self-actualization.

When I think people who are unstoppable, I think of fictional characters like the Six Million Dollar Man or the A-Team's Mr. T. They had purpose. A problem to solve each week, and an unflinching desire to come out on top. Similarly, a true innovator finds such purpose in their own problem-solving role, albeit a bit less violently.

Over the years myself, I've worked in banking, in risk, in insurance, in health care, and a number of other sectors, and I've been lucky to find a niche and purpose between two distinct worlds: business and technology. I enjoy being a bridge to patch the often disconnected conversation between these two seemingly disparate sides of the organization and find ways forward. As I've grown through my career, I've built credibility as a person who finds joy in what's normally a very complex and politically frustrating relationship between the business and technology elements of an organization.

The best organizations do all they can to allow people to find their purpose within a broad canvas of a job description or function—yet purpose is beyond the job mandate, beyond the job description. One of the great examples of this is "Google time," where employees are encouraged to spend 20 percent of their time on personal projects. In this way, Google is allowing employees to voluntarily pursue challenges and problems that don't normally fall under their job description. You probably know that Google Maps is now one of the most successful assets in Google's stable. What most people don't realize that Google Maps was originally a personal passion project borne out of "Google time."

An organization can't engineer purpose—they have to help people pursue their own interests as they evolve, and their purpose evolves with them. The best companies on the planet allow people to steal an outlet, to go beyond their job description, to dabble in areas of interest, areas that provide deeply satisfying fulfilment and self-actualization.

Finding Your Purpose

If you want to find your purpose—or your employees' purpose—in the innovation framework, you have to ask three key questions:

1. What am I passionate about as an individual? The answer is different for every single individual on this planet.

2. What can you be best at in the world? How do you define what you are number one at? Because the recognition of being the best at something can be a great driver of purpose. That could be something extremely niche—like being the best person at weaving coconut leaf baskets underwater in scuba gear. Regardless of how unique (or not) it is, the possibility of being the best at something helps imbue that pursuit with purpose.

3. Finally, if you can find something you're best at in the world, how can you make money doing that? This is extremely important to corporations, because it allows them to tie your own personal passion into their ability to make money, thereby justifying more time for you to spend on your purpose. If you're exploring an experimental new venture for your company and you can link that back to potential value over time, you're more likely to get ongoing support from that company.

Your purpose may have commercial strategic alignment to your employer, and if it does, that's potentially great for your employer. By facilitating this pursuit of purpose among their employees, allowing them to solve problems for the organization in a way that aligns with the company's commercial model, companies can boost their own bottom line as well as employee engagement and satisfaction.

However, an individual's purpose often may not have commercial strategic alignment to their employer's aims, and for a large percentage of corporations, having employees spending time on personal pet projects is not always a feasible use of company resources. In this case, that individual's purpose may be better exercised by branching out and creating their own startup. It's all part of the innovation process, of people finding their own place within the wider ecosystem.

Takeaways:
- For the individual, find your purpose, by discovering what you're best at; then work out how to make money from it
- For the organization, allow time for employees to find purpose, and direct it (where possible) to company endeavors

Purpose is where problem and passion come to a head. It's about an individual finding the one thing they're best equipped to do in the world, then aligning their energies so they can make that one thing their focus. From there, they have a powerful base of internal motivation and support for their problem-solving mission. To guide that mission, principles are crucial, and that's the final piece of the puzzle we'll talk about next.

Chapter 20
PRINCIPLES—THE CODE OF CONDUCT
AND HONOR FOR INNOVATION SOLDIERS

I 've been obsessed with Japanese culture since a very young age. I learned Japanese through primary and high school, and I've visited Japan several times. One of the aspects I admire in Japanese culture is that of the Japanese warrior—the samurai. A samurai is one who chooses to live his life according to a series of values, taken from a moral code of honor called Bushido, or the "way of the warrior." A samurai warrior would govern his life's directions based on the values he chose from the Bushido. They tended to pick those from the book which most suited them. You can learn a lot about being an Innovation Soldier from the samurai, for like the samurai, each innovation soldier must be principled in their struggle to innovate. The innovation soldier's principles are the final piece of the puzzle once problem, passion, and purpose are aligned.

In the Western world, it's very much like this if you're religious. If you're a Christian, one who goes by the Bible, you have the option of following thousands of possible guidelines—but few people will follow every one. It's probably not possible. They might choose four or five passages, or values that are very important to them; similarly, a samurai warrior would choose a handful of values that were important to them as an individual and they would seek perfection or enlightenment in that value.

You may have come across martial arts movies in which a warrior is doing calligraphy with a long brush (the kind that are three or four feet long). What they are trying to do is two things. First, long brush calligraphy helped them improve their sword craft—their ability to handle a sword. Second, the ultimate goal of this process was to find a new way to write the same character. The samurai was trying to be innovative, to find a new way of doing the same thing. That's how they practiced, how they constantly reconnected with their principles and this is the important part of having principles, you have to have a way to regularly reconnect with them, to remind yourself, to keep them front of mind so that when you do reach that tough decision they become your guidance.

In my case, I have six values chosen from the Bushido that have become my guiding principles, in both my personal and my professional life. Although I regard those values in their original Japanese, I'll give you the English words. They are:

- Courage
- Honor
- Wisdom
- Love
- Happiness
- Strength

When I was in Japan, back in 1999, I had a Japanese calligrapher put those six characters onto rice paper. I framed them, and to this day they sit on my study wall at home. They've been with me now for the better part of almost 20 years and continue to provide inspiration. Whenever I've met a milestone or a behavior in my life that I believed exemplified a certain value, I had the name of that value tattooed on my body, and the tattoos have grown over the years. The first one I got was at the age of 17, and the oldest I got very recently—they help me to remember the events that embody those principles, ones I used to govern my life.

Being principled is a foundation stone in guiding and creating repetitive innovation and entrepreneurship. Your core principles guide all your decisions, be they strategic decisions, resource allocation decisions, technology decisions, customer decisions, or pricing decisions, throughout the creation of whatever idea you are working on. Great principles define a lot of great individuals. Look at some of the greatest entrepreneurs of our time: Richard Branson, Mark Zuckerberg, Bill Gates. One of the common things they possess is a core set of principles that guide them. Consider the work the Bill and Melinda Gates Foundation is doing with malaria and financial inclusion. This work is based on a principle held by Bill Gates about the importance of creating positive impact on humanity. He does it because it's core to who he is and how he acts in the world.

These kinds of deeply embedded values define an entrepreneur beyond one or two ventures—they are principles that stick with them for life. In addition to his desire to have a positive impact on humanity, Bill Gates also possesses principles that have helped him succeed tremendously in business—principles that brought him great success at Microsoft, and which he's brought to the philanthropy world to ensure those endeavors are successful, as well. Steve Jobs, too, carried the same personal principles that helped him drive successful innovation at Apple, to Next Computers, to Pixar, and back to Apple again. Principles feed continuous innovative behavior and continuous innovation.

So the question is, do great innovators have certain principles in common? They sure do; some principles in business are universal, while others are more specific to the individual. I'll caveat that this is by no means an exhaustive list, one I'm sure can be added to or subtracted from.

Respect Customers and Employees

If you think about the shift from the industrial era to the digital area, in the current age a mutual empathy and appreciation for customers is one of the key traits of good entrepreneurs. Second to that is obviously you must have a common respect for employees—the people who are on either side help making your ideas happen deserve your respect. Fail to listen to either side at your peril.

Related to that is to define the potential commercial direction of the ventures you will *not* participate in. For instance, you might decide that not exploiting third world workers or children is an important principle. There's a growing number of organizations out there today who are becoming more and more principle-based. Companies like Body Shop. Lush. Fruit of the Loom. Adidas, Levis, and Country Road rate fairly well on these kinds of social goodness principles.

Or take a company like TOMS, with their One for One program. It originally began with shoes—for every pair sold, they donated a pair to help impoverished people in America and abroad. Today they provide funding for not only shoes, but sight initiatives, water programs, safe birth, and other services to people in need. These efforts were borne out of principles that originated as the founders' own principles and soon become part of the brand's DNA.

Be Transparent

Being transparent is a principle that can guide you to becoming a stronger entrepreneur. Think first of the opposite of transparency: opacity. Opaqueness prevents you from seeing and understanding. Transparency, on the other hand, allows you to see through and understand.

Transparency deals with looking at truth and honesty in the way we present the product or service, the way we solve problems—and how we see and treat ourselves. Today you'll find most innovation teams have transparency in some, but not every part of their product innovation process.

A transparent and honest dialogue between individuals and organizations provides much better understanding on both sides of the discussion and in turn results in better, more innovative products. People need to move from the position of being advocates of a specific solution, to being open facilitators of the best possible outcome. True open dialogue can be seen as the marriage of competing ideas and can result in a totally new idea that has the best elements of many ideas. Being transparent lets people see who you really are, and within the organization helps people really understand what's happening and let people see their own roles better.

Show Courage

Aristotle referred to courage as the first virtue, because it makes all of the other virtues possible. A leader, particularly in the innovation space, requires the courage to face the uncertainty that they or the business may not succeed. This leader must be willing to breed an organizational culture that accepts the risk of failure. Showing courage is risking defeat. It's all about being able to see the opportunities that exist in many of today's business challenges and actually being excited about those opportunities, instead of just being fearful of failure. It's recognizing that innovation projects by their very nature have uncertain outcomes. Despite the risk, despite the possibility of having your ideas shot down, an innovator has the courage to stand up and show how an idea can change the way the company does business, or perhaps even change the entire industry or the world.

Build Social Capital

Social capital as a principle helps build insight into every aspect of your company, industry, and beyond. Networking has always been regarded as a crucial skill in the business world, in both large and small organizations. In some industries, you can basically get hired based on the strength of your network. Innovators, especially, need to know how to network and communicate. When we're talking innovation—the broader and more varied the network, the better. The idea is that the wider your network, the more likely it is to be composed of diverse individuals from very different industries. It's great to build and maintain connections within your own industry, but an innovator needs to know what's going on across the board. As an innovator, you need to be exposed to different ways of thinking and doing things, of generating ideas and solving problems. Connections from other industries might just be the spark you need for some new ideas that can be applied to your business.

The other main reason for having a broad cross-industry network has to do with what we talked about in Chapter 15, enabling collaboration and innovation at the crossroads of industries. The lone genius tinkering away in their office, and arriving at a major breakthrough innovation on their own, does exist—Leonardo da Vinci or Alexander Graham Bell, for example—but increasingly, they're products of the past. Modern innovators, even people like Bill Gates or Steve Jobs, while driving forces of innovation, have innovated more precisely through collaboration. Innovation increasingly comes about through groups of people coming together to leverage their wide-ranging talents and knowledge to solve multifaceted challenges that cross multiple disciplines.

Be Adaptive

"Adapt or perish, now as ever, is nature's inexorable imperative." So said sci-fi great H. G. Wells. As with much in nature, it also applies to the business world.

If we flick back to a military example, in 2003, General Stanley McChrystal took command of the United States' Joint Special Operations Command (JSOC), an association of elite forces including the Navy SEALS, Army Rangers, and Delta Force. His mission: to defeat Al-Qaeda in Iraq. JSOC had the obvious advantage when it came to technology and resources. Yet a year later it was very clear they were losing. The reason? Because they were using an outdated organizational structure, one that prized efficiency, despite living in an era (and landscape) in which adaptability was key.

For decades, principles of efficiency were taught as gospel in business schools, and businesses thrived because of these principles, but with more information being shared at greater speeds, even today's most efficient organizations can't hope to keep up. The secret to success in today's world, instead, is adaptability. You've got to be smarter, and faster in the way you react. You need to let go of the idea that there is one "right way." Successful CEOs today know that the only constant is change, and that only companies that adapt to change will continue to survive. Whether you're at work, home or anywhere in between, we live in a fast-changing world, and you need to be adaptive.

On a personal level, think about it like this: when you acknowledge change as a constant and constantly keep adapting to that change, what you're doing is essentially keeping an open mind. It's impossible to adapt to what you cannot see. True innovators also understand that lessons from one arena can often be used to initiate innovation in another, so they usually do not limit their learning to just their own constricted field.

Do No Evil

We've spoken about the positive principles that guide innovators, but avoiding evil is just as important.

For a long time "Don't be evil" was the corporate slogan of Google. It's generally credited as coming from Google employee Paul Buchheit at a meeting to decide upon corporate values in early 2000. Buchheit, the creator of Gmail, said he "wanted something that, once you put it in there, would be hard to take out." This of course backfired a bit as there was a backlash in 2012 when Google began to track users universally across all its services—and "Don't be evil" is no longer so readily used at the company.

But having principles allows you to avoid distractions, seductions, and temptations. I'm returning to the religious analogy again, but it does work in the same way that someone might refer to any religious book to keep them on the straight and narrow. I'm not saying that corporations are always evil or expect you to do evil, but it's very easy to find a shortcut to exploit employees, suppliers, or collaborators—when you are principle based, that should guide you away from easy, but potentially exploitative, shortcuts in your business or personal life.

Principles provide guidance to the decision points in your life. These principles will help you magnify both your purpose and passion, particularly over long periods of time. And when you have someone dangling an attractive carrot that you know will offer only short-term return, this is where your principles will help you say no: "I don't want to take the short term bet. I want us to stick with my long-term principles, values, and goals." The challenge here is it's very individual. Principles are very important to an individual's identity and their character and path to get closer to self-actualization.

In the corporate innovation space, it's also important to get to know the principles of those people around you, particularly if you going to innovate with them. By understanding their principles, particularly in the context of Maslow's Hierarchy of Needs, or even the stories behind that make those principles real (like my Bushido story), you begin to appreciate and understand someone's perspective and the underlying psychology of their decision-making framework. If somebody's going to be uncomfortable with something based on their principles, it's better knowing ahead of time, before you even get to that scenario.

Understanding individuals around you is particularly useful in challenging scenarios—which are very common in the innovation space. If we go back to the Innovation Wars analogy for a moment, military teams, and particularly platoons, tend to know each other intimately. They know about other platoon members' families, they know what's important to each other, they know what religion each person follows or doesn't, they know what guides you, what quotes are important to you, where you went to school. They have to know these things, because knowing the people around you well is critical to breeding trust in dangerous situations.

Take the example of the Navy Seals who were sent to Pakistan to take out Bin Laden. This was a team that was very isolated for the duration of their operation. As a result, the team members had to possess an extremely high level of trust in and reliance on each other, and that comes out of knowing each other's principles. When shit hits the fan—you want to know what's going to guide the decisions of everybody around you.

Fighting an innovation war is intrinsically a courageous task. For individuals, that means finding your principles and living by them. For organizations, it means finding people who align to your principles. It will present many decision points for the innovation soldier, some foreseen and others unexpected, which will test that person's resolve. The central principle of courage, as well as others like transparency, respect, and adaptability, help to light the path and solidify the soldier's purpose.

CONCLUSION

"Nothing wilts faster than laurels that have been rested upon."
—Percy Bysshe Shelley

Today, a number of key industries are under threat: financial services, media, insurance, healthcare, education, and many more. At the same time, many organizations that have been innovative in the past have shown a limited ability to respond to the market in the digital economy. Incumbency doesn't guarantee a golden ticket to the future. To amplify this reality, it can take just weeks, not years, of inaction to be disrupted.

The key for incumbent organizations facing these risks is to build a bridge from where they are today to where they want to be in the future. At my company, Innovation Labs, we work with other organizations to help them use the four Cs to build this bridge and chart their own innovation journey. This process guides companies along the transformational path they must take if they want to approach a more innovative state, by giving them a framework to generate and test ideas, to identify which ones can be turned into solutions that address real customer needs and problems.

Along the way, we help these companies must approach the idea generation and development process as strategically as possible. Some of the ideas that emerge will grow into viable business opportunities while others will likely fail, and the company needs to manage these possibilities like a portfolio of strategic options, each of which has its own growth/value curve that justifies potential investment. As ideas pass through the various stages of development, the company needs to have a firm grasp of the entry and exit criteria for these ideas in order to make smart decisions on when to invest and when to kill them. Also, throughout the entire process from initial idea to prototyping, we use data and metrics to give us an objective way of measuring the potential value of each idea or solution as it evolves. Finally, our system also emphasizes the fact that some things must die for new ideas to flourish. Truly innovative transformation must include consideration for the components of the current business that require replacement as new options grow to viable scale.

Going Behind the Scenes

What does this process look like? I'll take you through the process through which we help companies become skilled at idea generation and development from a high level.

The first stage is to set the right **Context**. We sit down with the company's stakeholders and have an open discussion around the questions, "Where are you today? Are you aware of your current strengths? Your current weaknesses? Current opportunities in the market? The threats that are coming on the horizon?" From there, we craft a clear statement as to where the company would like to be in three to five years, not just in terms of products or services, but the value they create in the market.

That puts the organization is a kind of aspirational state, in which it can clarify its priorities for the next twelve months. As part of this process, we identify which components of the organization are most vulnerable right now. What are the critical problems that need to be addressed within the organization? Where is the organization most threatened? Then, we work on prioritizing the top two or three of those issues to tackle first.

Next, we move into **Culture**. We use learning sessions to train a workforce on the culture that is going to lay the foundations for how it will operate in the future. This includes all the things we mentioned in the Culture chapter: curiosity, experimentation, and acceptance of failure.

Today, we do this as a three-day workshop guided by our Head of Learning and Development of HR, who is equipped to guide our client company in how to deploy new skills and a new culture in their organization. Every person who completes that workshop receives a "license" affirming that they are now trained in the new culture of the organization.

As part of this process, people break off into "pods" that generate their own ideas. These pods represent the earliest form of a unit that could eventually become an entirely new business unit in the company.

We start by having each pod think about the customer problems they would solve today if they had completely free rein. Answering this question also helps identify which members of the workforce are best equipped to build solutions to those problems. Your best chance of succeeding is to work on customer problems your people are already aware of—and the people who are best able to identify those problems are those who speak to your customers every single day: customer service staff, front-line sales people, and others in similar roles.

In this way, the pods are set up to identify the problems that are worth solving, the ones with the greatest potential for addressing a known opportunity in the market.

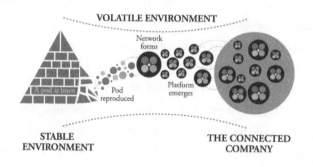

That's when we move on to **Capability**. We take one or two ideas, or even five, depending on budgets. Then, we help the team execute on those ideas.

We usually hold a five-day group camp that's part educational, part practical where they learn skills and frameworks like design thinking, persona ideation, and the lean startup model—but also apply them at the same time. We coach them through the process of answering these questions: "If you had a new idea to work on, what are the tools and frameworks that you would apply to execute on that idea? In what order? And over what period of time? What does success look like? What is the sample price you pay at the sample size you would use as part of the experiments?" Also, at the end of that, sometimes five days they pitch back to the organization an answer to the key question, "Should we build a solution to this problem?"

This gives people their first practice of building momentum, gathering support from stakeholders, and communicating the value of an opportunity within the organization, but it still happens on a very small level and over a short period of time (five days). It's also not a process that provides these teams with full rein; there's still an element of oversight, in that the individuals who go through this process must have first gone through the cultural training program and earned their "license"; identified a customer problem they want to solve; and gone through the boot camp process to apply their newfound skills to that idea.

From there, if the problem is one that the organization wants to solve, we'll move to the prototyping phase to create a minimum viable version of the solution that can be tested. In parallel, we are also engaged in customer development. The typical time frame for this part of the process is about twelve weeks. In the prototyping phase, larger pods start to emerge as smaller pods come together and become like multiple cells of a single organism—starting to form the new business units that will eventually become an entirely new organization.

The Courage to Adapt

In today's cutthroat corporate world, no company may be safe—but no company is doomed either. Large companies like Apple, Google, Ford, and IKEA have shown that they can still be innovative.

They do this by creating a context and culture of innovation, developing the organizational capabilities that will drive innovation, and collaborating with outside partners to magnify their capacity for innovation.

They look to the startup model for ideas on being lean and agile, on developing solutions and products in a user-centered and user-led manner.

They seek out and embrace leaders who possess the traits of successful innovators: passion, vision, collaboration, leadership, failure acceptance, embracing change, storytelling, thinking big.

They look for and and cultivate innovation soldiers with the right qualities. They find people with a fit for the problems the organization is trying to solve, who will be passionate about solving them, who can rally themselves to a greater purpose in pursuit of those solutions, and who will fight this war guided by a set of invincible principles.

Then they put it all together—they understand that true innovation is not a project, or an optics play, but a courageous undertaking that requires multiple layers and pieces to come together.

And finally, they commit to making this whole process a continuous one— to not resting on their laurels—by reevaluating their whole innovation model in light of the constant change that defines every industry today.

I hope this book has given you, the aspiring innovator, some insights to get started adopting the mindset and building the frameworks to successfully fight your own innovation war. As your embark on this war, remember that how successful you've been, how successful you are, and how successful you may be are three entirely different things that mustn't be confused. Perhaps you're a successful company in a dying industry. Are you doing something truly innovative to set yourself apart from the pack, or is it just a matter of time until the bell tolls for you? Even if you are doing something different, that may still not be enough, because today's *innovative* may be tomorrow's *irrelevant*. What is your vision of success going forward? Is it through doing the same thing? Because chances are, that's not going to work.

Thankfully, you have a wealth of tools and raw materials at your disposal to win your war. The combination of increasingly accessible technologies and frameworks, along with the democratization of education, presents a huge opportunity for large organizations seeking to innovate. There are immensely powerful tools and frameworks available to just about anyone—the lean startup model, agile, social media, open source programming, public cloud, and much more—along with the growing ability for people to learn these skills and many, many others from anywhere at anytime.

This new reality can be a boon to your innovation war if you use it to your advantage. Create an environment—lay the groundwork of context and culture—then identify the skills and capabilities you need your workforce to have in order to win that war—lean on that workforce to identify those skills and capabilities. Make it clear that you support their desire to learn, and take full advantage of the new level playing field that has made the tools of innovation more accessible than ever.

The playing field has leveled within the organization too. In a similar way, lean on your workforce to identify the problems—and therefore the solutions—that will make a true difference to your market. Gone are the days of CEOs pontificating in their corner offices about what the company needs to make next. Now it's the companies that tap into their soldiers on their frontlines, the ones who are face-to-face with customers and dealing with the daily realities of your industry, who are best positioned to tell you what needs to be fixed and what needs to be built.

If your organization's appetite for the upheaval of internal transformation is not strong, then maybe a model like corporate venture capital (CVC) or an innovation lab is right for you. Create a siloed framework for innovation adjacent to the organization, then unleash it. Whatever you do, don't forget the spirit of introspection that goes with every step in the innovation of the process. Fighting and winning an innovation war is about constant questioning and constant learning. What needs to change internally? What companies are out there in your industry or beyond that can you learn from? Be willing to constantly ask if you're innovating or merely engaging in innovation theater.

Understand, Create, Enable, Continue

The first step for any organization is understanding at an honest level where you are today. You can drive a lot of this awareness by doing the simple SWOT analysis from Chapter 4. If you can identify your strengths and weaknesses, as well as the opportunities and threats out there in your industry, you'll have accomplished the critical first step to preparing to win your innovation war.

The second step is to start the process of understanding what value creation for your organization might look like in five years, then reverse engineering that in a way to set the priorities for the next one to two years.

This step requires courage, because it's highly likely that greater than 50 percent of your current operating model will have to change. Everything else is about establishing navigational tactics, strategic tactics, working models of frameworks, but the overarching element is knowing where you are today, where you have to be in five years' time to survive and thrive, and what are going to be the key priorities in the next twelve to twenty-four months that will put you on the path toward success.

The third step is to lay the groundwork within the organization—creating the context, culture, capabilities, and collaborative engagements to make innovation happen.

The fourth step is to identify and empower the people who fit the problems facing the organizations, who will pursue solutions with passion, purpose, and principles.

The fifth step is a meta-step, because this process is not linear but cyclical. It must be renewed and repeated over time through continuous self-awareness and reevaluation.

Putting it all together:

1. Understand What Is Now: Develop a Deep Awareness of Yourself and Your Industry
2. Understand What Is Possible: Where Can You Go From Here?
3. Create the Environment—Context, Culture, Capability, and Collaboration
4. Enable Your People—Problem, Passion, Purpose, and Principles
5. Continue the Cycle

But the most important and missing step is to **recognize** that your innovation war has already started, and that it's time to join the fray. It pays to remember the definition of "startup" offered by two business leaders we met back in Chapter 6. As Warby Parker's Neil Blumenthal put it, "a startup is a company working to solve a problem where the solution is not obvious and success is not guaranteed." And as Homejoy's Adora Cheung defines it, a startup is simply a "state of mind." These definitions together encapsulate not just the spirit of the startup, but the spirit of the innovator in general, the person or organization that's willing to persist in uncertainty and drive toward solutions that may not be apparent. To be constantly willing to change the way things are and create something new.

ABOUT THE AUTHOR

A technology guru, Scott Bales is a global leader in the cutting edge arena known as "The Digital Shift," encompassing innovation, culture, design, technology and mobility in a world gone digital. A thought leader through and through, Scott thrives on the intersection between cultural and behavioral changes in the face of technology innovations.

The MD of advisory firm Innovation Labs Asia, Scott worked previously as Chief Mobile Officer for Moven, the world's first-ever digital everyday bank. Described as a "Digital Warrior," Scott has found a way to successfully mesh his fascination with people and what motivates them together with a raw enthusiasm for technology.

In a world where technology reigns, you must practice what you preach, and Scott does exactly that. He's founding member of Next Bank, mentor to Entrepreneurs across the world on Lean Startup, sits on the Board of Care Pakistan and holds advisory positions at Publishizer, FastaCash, Our Better World, The HUB Singapore and Apps 4 Good. He's a man on a mission to transform mainstream thought processing around conventional business practices.

Scott has appeared at TEDx, Social Media Week, Google Think, Fund Forum, Asian Banker, Next Money and a long list of private events. His thought leadership has appeared in WIRED, Australian Financial Review and E27.